KING JOEY

Enjoy!

KING JOEY

Upfront and Personal

Joe Harper
with Charlie Allan

BIRLINN

This edition first published in 2008 by
Birlinn Limited
West Newington House
10 Newington Road
Edinburgh
EH9 1QS

www.birlinn.co.uk

ISBN 13: 978 1 84158 767 7

British Library Cataloguing-in-Publication Data
A catalogue record for this book is available from the British Library

Designed and typeset by Iolaire Typesetting, Newtonmore
Printed and bound by Clays Ltd, St Ives plc

To my parents and my children,
whom I love more than life itself.

CONTENTS

CONTENTS

ACKNOWLEDGEMENTS

❖

To Janice Allan, Charlie's wife, for the loan of her husband over the first few months of 2008.

Thanks also to Jim Strachan for his proofreading and editorial skills.

At the *Evening Express*, thanks to editor Damian Bates, librarians Bob Stewart and Duncan Smith, and to Alan Paterson and Callum Main of the picture desk.

First, the Final Whistle

'That's when what had transpired hit me with full force'

My last day as a player with Aberdeen Football Club ended with me shedding buckets of tears because I had been booted out, like a scrap of rubbish, by the club for which I had scored a record 205 goals. I was crowned King of the Beach End by the Aberdeen fans because of my scoring exploits during two spells with the club, starting in 1969 and ending in 1981.

I'm sure it will surprise many of my subjects to learn that my final day as a player for the Dons ended with the legendary Alex Ferguson more or less banishing me from Pittodrie Stadium, without so much as a thank-you for my services to the club. I will never forgive him for that, and I will also not forgive Fergie for the character assassination carried out on me in his autobiography, released many years after we had worked together at Aberdeen. Fergie, the manager, I admire. His record of success with Aberdeen and Manchester United demands that. But Fergie, the man, is a different matter, of which there will be more later. Suffice it to say for the present that I have not been able to figure out why Fergie came to hate me so much. All I ever did was try to score as many goals as I could for him at Aberdeen. While preparing this record of my life, I have tried to seek out what it was that I did to Fergie that made him feel compelled to write such awful things about me in 1999. He even wrote that he was happy I had suffered a career-threatening injury, so I suppose it should have been no surprise that we were barely on speaking terms when he asked me to call at his office at Pittodrie on a sunny day in May 1981. I had spent the 1980-81 campaign battling to recover from a knee injury suffered in a Scottish League Cup clash with Celtic in 1979. I was 33, but like most players I was sure that I would win my fitness battle and be able to make a further contribution to the Dons, perhaps as back-up to Mark McGhee, who had used my absence to his advantage and had become the first-choice striker at the club. Alex Ferguson had other ideas.

The rift between player and manager had become as wide as the Grand Canyon because of what happened the summer before, after the Dons had celebrated achieving their first league title since 1955. The injury against Celtic meant that I was unable to take part in that glorious league campaign beyond November, but I had appeared in sufficient matches to qualify for a winners' medal. I was delighted because it meant that I had completed the domestic treble with the Dons, having won the Scottish Cup with them in 1970 and League Cup in 1976. The thought of getting my hands on that medal kept me going through all the painful rehabilitation work required to build up my shattered knee. It is humiliating then to relate that I had practically to beg for that medal.

The Dons clinched the title with a 5-0 win over Hibernian at Easter Road in May 1980. It was disappointing not to be invited to watch that game, given that it meant so much to those of us who had devoted the bulk of their careers to Aberdeen. I had undergone a series of operations on my knee and was not long out of plaster, which meant that I was not fit to travel to Edinburgh under my own steam. I would have jumped at the chance to be present at Easter Road to offer encouragement to the lads and to soak up the atmosphere on what proved to be a day that no Dons fan will forget. Unfortunately, I had to be content with watching highlights of the game on television back in Aberdeen that night. It gladdened my heart to see old pals Bobby Clark and Drew Jarvie – who had been with me at the club since the early 1970s – celebrating what was the highlight of all our careers. Joe Harper, however, was not invited to any of the celebrations after the game or to the homecoming parade in Aberdeen held on the following day. I can only assume that other players received their medals at some sort of ceremony, because I was not invited to that either.

Some months later, I overheard some of the lads talking about how inspiring it was to hold a league-winners' medal in their hands. I was entitled to a medal and believed that the club for which I had amassed so many goals would not forget me, at the very least. It saddened me that ultimately I was forced to swallow my pride and visit the office of club secretary Ian Taggart to ask for my medal. 'I will have to go and check if you qualify for one,' said Taggart, a little man who had the look of a rat about him to my eyes, and who was disliked by many people at the club. He left me standing in front of his desk, like a guilty schoolboy, while he scurried along the corridor to Fergie's office. He returned a couple of minutes later and stated in a manner that suggested he was not exactly pleased: 'It appears you can get one, after all.' Taggart reached into a drawer of his desk, picked out a boxed medal and chucked it in my direction . . . which was hardly the way that I had pictured receiving what remains one of my most prized possessions. I was furious, but there was little point in taking Taggart to task, for he was little more than a go-for, and I was not surprised when he was axed by the Dons a few years later.

That unfortunate incident made me even more determined to

make a comeback, and to play so well for Aberdeen that it would be impossible for anyone to treat me with as little respect as Fergie and his lackey Taggart had shown that day. It was a hard slog because I had been told at one stage that the knee injury could finish my career, but I have never been a quitter and pushed myself harder than ever in an effort to get fit, hoping that Fergie would renew my contract, which was due to expire in July 1981.

My spirits were raised when I eventually made it back into the first team for the league game versus Kilmarnock at Pittodrie in May. We lost 2-0 watched by just 6,300 fans, but I was clinging to the hope that the manager would grant me the opportunity to end my Aberdeen career on a high. My hopes were dashed when club trainer Teddy Scott, a marvellous character who rightly received a testimonial against Fergie's Manchester United in 1999, entered the dressing-room and told me that the gaffer wished to see me. The instant I entered his office and saw that the manager's assistant Archie Knox was present too, I realised that this would not amount to a pleasant conversation. Alex Ferguson avoided eye contact, which confirmed my misgivings, and he declared bluntly: 'I'm not renewing your contract.' The words hit me like a punch in the gut, but I had been in the game long enough to realise that time waits for no man, even one who can flourish goal-scoring records. I had been out of action for more than a year and a half because of a serious injury, and Fergie was the executive who was paid to decide if I was still up to the task. He thought not, and I had to respect his verdict, though it was hard to hide the hurt that I felt. But worse was to come from Fergie's lips: 'I don't want to ever see you back in here again. Get your boots on the way out: the rest of your wages will be sent to you.' So ended my career with Aberdeen Football Club.

❖

I was so stunned by the experience that I can barely remember the next few minutes. I certainly do not recall receiving so much as a thank-you from Alex Ferguson for my contribution to the club over the years. I cannot criticise the man for letting me go, but to attempt to banish me from the club that I loved, and to leave me feeling like some sort of criminal, cut me to the quick. I eventually returned to the dressing-room, and my expression was sufficiently grim to prompt Alex McLeish – a young defender who would assume the status of Aberdeen legend and prove to be an outstanding manager – to inquire: 'What's happened to you, wee man?' I responded with: 'That's me finished.' I propped the back of my head against the wall and closed my eyes tight to stem any tears; I feared that looking at my lost colleagues would prompt me to break down completely. 'I've been told to get out now, and never come back.' Young Alex attempted to offer some support by commenting: 'If that's the way they treat you, how are they going to treat the rest of us?' But I was too caught up in private agony to acknowledge his attempts to comfort me, and I was still in a daze when the odious Taggart delivered a black plastic bag into which I placed my four pairs of boots, which had been selected for use according to pitch and weather conditions.

I'm certainly not ashamed to admit that I was shedding tears of bitterness and disappointment as I walked from the stadium for the last time as a Don. I was determined not to show how upset I was, for grown men from Greenock are not supposed to blubber like babies over something like losing a job. I took a big breath, started the car and began to drive home to deliver the bad news to my wife and family. I made the fundamental mistake of glancing in the rear-view mirror in which was reflected the image of Pittodrie, an arena which had served as my spiritual home for much of my adult life. That poignant picture was receding into the distance, and that's when what had transpired hit me with full force. The tears began to flow so intensely that I was forced to park the car by the side of the road. I slumped over the steering wheel, and let it all out. To be sure, the despair that I was feeling because my days as a Don were over was mixed with anger over the cold-hearted way in which Fergie had blown the final whistle. When I read his book years later, it was clear that he had no intention of keeping me on board, so he could have handled my departure with some subtlety at least. It particularly angers me that he did not deliver the bad news before I played in that last game against Kilmarnock. The pain of departure would not have been any less, but I would have been allowed to bid a proper farewell to the Dons fans, who had done so much to boost my spirits throughout my career. I'm also sure that the game would have attracted more than 6,300 spectators if it had been billed as Joe Harper's swansong.

Alex Ferguson obviously did not do that, and he had also pushed me into exile. Word filtered back to me over the next few weeks that I would not be welcome at Pittodrie in *any* capacity while he was in charge. That was underlined when I attempted to acquire tickets, which I offered to buy, to attend a big European match with my son a couple of years later. I was told by phone that my request would have to be cleared by the manager, and also that the club's record top-scorer would not be allowed to purchase tickets unless he had collected enough vouchers, just like any Aberdeen supporter. It was not until I set eyes on Fergie's biography that I understood why that happened. The man, for reasons known to himself, despises me.

I hope that this account will convince the reader that Alex Ferguson had no justification for treating me in the manner that he did. I loved playing for Aberdeen, and I had dreamed of a farewell that would see me warmly applauding the fans who had made my time at Pittodrie so special. I could not have envisaged that the last day would end with me whimpering like a child yards from the place where I had scored so many goals, and had created so many happy memories. It took me more than 20 minutes to regain my composure sufficiently to drive home. And yet, while being comforted by my family I finally came to accept that I was still one of the luckiest men alive, whatever my former manager might think. Thanks to football, I had seen the world, played for my country and in cup finals, and scored goals for my beloved Aberdeen and Morton as well as for Huddersfield Town, Everton, Hibs and Scotland. I had made many friends and enjoyed wonderful experiences along the way. In short, I had not done too badly for a tubby wee boy fae Greenock, whose parents once despaired about what the future might hold for their only child.

2

GREENOCK'S BOY WONDER

'Now I understand how serious polio can be,
I realise that I was very lucky'

There was a time during my childhood when it was feared that I would never walk again, let alone stride ahead to become a professional footballer. Joseph Montgomery Harper came into this world on 11 January 1948. People ask if the Montgomery was given to me as a tribute to the British general who was a national hero in the Second World War in which my father fought. I'm proud to inform them that I was named after my true hero, my maternal grandfather, who was also Joseph. His mother's maiden name was Montgomery. Grandad Joe was my John Wayne, a colossus of a man and the one who gave me the best advice any striker will ever receive. 'Joe,' he said as I prepared for one of my earliest schoolboy matches, 'most goal-keepers wear yellow jerseys. So when the ball comes to you, just aim it at the yellow target. If you miss it, it will be a goal. If you don't, it will be a save, and people will say you at least got the shot on target.' Simple words, but advice that I followed throughout my playing career. Sadly, Grandad Joe died when I was with Huddersfield and still attempting to make my name in the game. It hurts that he did not share in the success that I enjoyed at Aberdeen, and that he did not see me score for Scotland, but I like to think he is up there somewhere looking down with pride because I put his words of advice to good use.

Like my grandfather and my father Eddie, I'm a Greenock man who is proud of his roots, though the burgh on the Clyde in which I was brought up was markedly different to the town that bears the name today. In the late 1940s the citizens of Greenock, like so many throughout Europe, were making the best of coping with the after-effects of a terrible war. My father was a soldier in that war. He was involved in the key Battle of Anzio in Italy and served in Egypt and France, though he rarely reveals much detail about that period of his life. He met my mother Margaret during the early years of the war, and he was off to the conflict before they had had a chance to enjoy a honeymoon. Not that they could have travelled far. Times were tough for a young married couple in Greenock, and even tougher with a new mouth to feed. Like many Greenock men, my father worked in the shipyards; he was a plater with Scott's, and says they were the men who built the first nuclear submarines. My father left the house at 6.30 a.m. to walk three miles to his place of work, and he was lucky if he was home again by 5.30 p.m. All for a bulging weekly pay packet of three pounds and ten shillings, which equates to £3.50 in decimal currency. My mother did her bit to make ends meet by working in a factory that made hessian sacks to carry coal. They were a hard-working couple, and I can honestly say that I did not want for anything throughout my childhood.

My health took a turn for the worse, though, when I was seven years old. I was too young to remember all the details, but my mother told me that she was concerned when I became increasingly ill over a period of days. Eventually I was so bad that I could not walk, and I was promptly removed to hospital in Glasgow, where I was diagnosed as suffering from polio.

The disease, which was virtually wiped in later years, comes in various forms. Unfortunately it was discovered that I had the worst type, known as paralytic polio, which attacks the nerves that help to control limb muscles and the respiratory system. Indeed my parents were warned there was a real chance that I might never walk again. At the very least my limbs were expected to be weakened, even withered, and that would clearly have affected my chances of participating in sport.

I was confined to the hospital in Glasgow for four months, and I can recall being afraid because I couldn't even get out of bed, and I had been placed in a ward full of adults. In the next bed was a policeman, who was more seriously ill than the laddie fae Greenock, and I cannot forget how that man – whose name, I regret, I cannot recall – ignored his own problems in an effort to make a frightened child feel a bit more comfortable. It was difficult for my parents to travel the distance from our home to the heart of Glasgow, as we had no car and public transport was not so rapid as it is these days, but the police-man's wife compensated for that by using some of her visiting time to speak to me, and she made sure I had everything I needed. She even brought in toys and sweets for the young patient. I made a gradual improvement, though I was still a bit unsteady on my feet when I was finally allowed out of bed. I was missing my precious football, which I had not been allowed to take into hospital, but the policeman sorted that by making one out of rolled-up newspapers. He spent hours encouraging me from his sick bed as I built up my strength by playing keepy-up and dribbling about the ward with my im-provised ball. It worked a treat, because I was soon back home and playing with my pals again as if nothing had happened. It must have been a very worrying time for my parents, however. Now I understand how serious polio can be, I realise that I was very lucky.

I was also fortunate when I accidentally swallowed some bleach at the age of four. I was playing at a relative's house, a bottle was left within my reach, and I assumed it was lemonade and began to drink it down. Thankfully I was spotted and hurried off to hospital, where my stomach was pumped clean. I have only a vague memory of that incident, which is perhaps a good thing. My recovery from both childhood predicaments was aided by the fact that I was brought up in a very loving home environment, and I feel blessed to be able to say that in the year that I celebrate my 60th birthday, both my parents are alive and well. My life has been devoted to making them proud and to feeling that the sacrifices they made on my behalf were worthwhile.

❖

My earliest childhood memories are of us staying in the old Nissen huts in Boyd Street, which have long since been demolished. Reports from that time described the accommodation as 'a clearance of the slums', but I have nothing but fond memories of that first family home. The huts had arched, corrugated-iron roofs and each was divided into four sections to cater for four families. Each home contained just one bedroom and a living-room. They had no electricity – it was a time of gas lighting, outside toilets and little in the way of privacy – and I still shiver when I recall sitting in cold water in a big tin bath in front of the coal fire. My mother washed all our clothes by hand, and she extracted the last drops of water from the wool or cotton material by using an old-fashioned mangle.

Despite the privations and shortages, a great sense of community was evident in the area, with everyone looking after everyone else. One treat came as a result of living beside a sugar factory, the other industry for which Greenock was noted. The refinery discarded big solid chunks of sugar that were not suitable for processing, and the local kids took them home for a good *sook*. These surplus chunks lasted for hours until there was nothing left to *sook,* and I enjoyed the treats as much as any more expensive sweets that I could afford later in life.

When the huts were demolished, we lodged with Grandad Joe for a spell before moving to a council tenement in Finnieston Street. It was six to a close, and we stayed in the bottom-right flat. I got a bedroom to myself, which was one of the advantages of being an only child when many families had to make space for five or six. Our tenement was like one big happy family. The Morrisons' house was across the landing and Ian Lafferty and his family were upstairs. One of my earliest pals was Ian Moran, who lived across the street. He was my right-hand man, and we went almost everywhere together. I have not kept in touch with Ian as much as I would have liked, though I was delighted to see that he was still doing well when our paths crossed in recent years.

My closest pal from those days was John Morrison. As well as playing together, John and I boosted our pocket-money by helping to deliver milk and rolls. It meant an early start on school days, but we had so many laughs we didn't mind. Our main passion, of course, was football. Like most youngsters in those days, Ian, John and I played for hours on end in the street outside our homes, all day, every day. We used jackets or lamp-posts to mark the goals, and were not interested in other leisure pursuits. That form of street football has died because almost every family owns a car nowadays. It was different in Greenock in the 1950s, when we could play for long spells and rarely see a car, never mind having to avoid vehicles parked on our 'pitch'. Those games helped to hone the skills that were to serve me so well in later years: you would be a defender one minute, then a goalie, then play as a striker. It was scoring goals that mattered most to me, and I got as much joy out of bashing them in between two jackets as I did rippling real goal-nets later. Without wishing to boast, I was one of the best players in the area, but I wasn't *the* best. That honour belonged to . . . Dorothy Miller. I can honestly say that I have yet to see a boy play football better than she did at that age. We just could not get the ball off Dorothy at times, and it's a shame she did not enjoy the opportunities that are open to female players these days. I lost touch with Dorothy as we got older, which is a shame. I wonder what became of her?

I attended Belville Primary School, which has long since been demolished, and we played football there for much of the time. I wouldn't say that I hated school, but I longed for the bell to signal the end of the day and the chance to get back on the streets to play at being our heroes of the day.

My favourite was the legendary Brazilian striker Pele, who inflamed my desire to become a footballer with his amazing exploits at the 1958 World Cup finals in Sweden. I watched his performance as the Brazilians beat the hosts 5-2 in the final in grainy black and white on a neighbour's telly, and it was enough to convince me that playing in the World Cup was what I wanted to do. For the present I had to be content with playing for Mount Secondary School on Saturday mornings and the Boys' Brigade in the afternoons. I had little chance to follow my local senior side Morton, but like most Greenock lads I was happy to say that they were my team. Given that I was to make my name as a striker, it's strange that my biggest local heroes of that time were goalkeepers for Morton. Jimmy Cowan, of course, was already a Morton legend, and I was hooked on all the stories I heard about him. I was fortunate to meet Jimmy once, late in his life, at a charity function, and I recall being star-struck at finally speaking to the great man. The other goalie that I idolised was an

Irishman named Finbar Flood, and I believe that he went on to do well for himself with the Guinness company. Sadly I have not experienced the pleasure of meeting Finbar, but I took in every word of his exploits with Morton via much-cherished copies of the Glasgow *Evening Times Pink*, which was a must for football fans before television and radio coverage and the Internet ruled the roost.

The odd chances I got to see Morton perform stir happy memories of my mother giving me two shillings and sixpence (12 pence in today's money) to cover the cost of entry to Cappielow and some sweets. What she didn't know was that I used the money to buy chips for me and my pals; I have to admit that we clambered over the wall of the stadium and cheated our way in. My career as a master fraudster soon came unstuck, however. I was about to climb over the perimeter one day when a man came up and asked if I knew of a way to get into the stadium for nothing. Being the helpful sort, I showed him our secret entry point, only to discover that he was a policeman sent to stop rogues like me robbing Morton of their deserved spectator income. I was taken to the police station and thought I had been let off with a lecture, and scurried off home. But the police had already been to see my parents, and I was fined the sum of £1 for my heinous crime.

My parents, thankfully, did not stop me playing or watching football. They could see it was the passion of my life. The first adult match that I recall going to see was at Hampden Park in Glasgow, and it was the 1960 Scottish Junior Cup final between Greenock Juniors and St Andrews. I went with my father and my grandfather, and it seemed as if the whole of Greenock had turned out to cheer on the local side. Billy Brabender, captain of my Boys' Brigade company, played for Greenock, so I was very excited, and despite St Andrews winning by 3-1, I left Hampden dreaming about returning some day to score the winning goal in a final. My hopes of achieving that were bolstered by discovering the knack of cracking in the goals, lots of them, for my school and the BB team. I received lots of encouragement from Alistair McDonald, the English teacher, who maintained that I possessed genuine talent and urged me to stick in and to practise hard after school. That was more than could be said of gym teacher Andy Harvey, who was more into cricket and rugby, but I took note of Mr McDonald's view, and recall being the toast of Mount School for claiming seven strikes in a 12-1 victory over arch-rivals St Mary's. It was during those happy schooldays that I first experienced the joy of winning trophies. I triumphed in cup finals while at primary and secondary school, and such achievements added fire to my desire to gain more successes in the game I love. My father, who was a boxing champion in the army, encouraged me all the way, but my grandfather, a real football man, was the most powerful driving force. I cannot recall him missing any game in which I played.

Joseph Montgomery Harper was not the only young striker from Greenock beginning to make his mark. Eddie Morrison, who went on to score 121 goals in 268 appearances for Kilmarnock as well as becoming manager at Rugby Park, was earning rave reviews for his exploits with St Columba's School. I still see a fair bit of Eddie and enjoy winding him up about the day we went head to head in a school cup final. Eddie was unstoppable in the first half, scoring a hat-trick to give his team what looked like a winning 3-0 lead. For some reason, which neither of us has been able to work out, the guy running St Columba's decided to move Eddie into their defence for the second half, to man-mark me. I also scored a hat-trick and we won 4-3, which pretty much sums up why Eddie did not develop into a star defender at Rugby Park. It was a friendly rivalry, though, and Eddie and I relished the chance to play together for the Greenock and District School Select.

We worked well together, as we proved when we went to Dundee and fought back from 4-0 down to win 5-4 with Eddie scoring three and me getting the other two. Both of us had been mentioned in the *Greenock Telegraph*, which meant a lot to local kids, but my desire to play football any time, any place, almost cost me my dream of going professional.

I had been told that I was certain to be picked for the Scotland Schoolboy Select, which was seen as a stepping-stone towards being spotted and fixed up with a senior club. Before the squad were named I decided to watch one of my pals Dave Kane play for Port Glasgow Rangers against Port Glasgow Rovers, who were in the local juvenile league. When we arrived at Park Lea, Port Glasgow, we discovered that Dave's team were two players short. I was only 15 and a bit young to be playing in what was mainly an under-18 league, but jumped at the chance when I was asked if I wanted to help to make up the numbers. It was a friendly game, so I saw it as no more than a glorified kick-about anyway. I had to borrow a pair of boots, but scored two goals in a 4-0 result. I thought nothing more about it until the following Friday when the *Greenock Telegraph* carried a small report on the game highlighting the outstanding play by 'a young Greenock striker called Joe Harper'. The next thing I experienced was Mr Harvey, my nemesis from school, scolding me for taking part in the game. Unknown to me, laddies were not allowed to play schools *and* juvenile football, but luckily I had not breached any rules because the game was a friendly, and I did not have to be registered. Mr Harvey had seen his chance to take me down a peg or two, and the verbal bashing was punishment enough, but the gym teacher, a large man who seemed at his happiest when he was upsetting me, decided that a firmer line was needed. He told me to forget any thoughts of playing for Scotland, and he rejected the request for me to join the squad. I was heartbroken. Playing for my country, at any level, was something I dearly wanted to do, and I never forgave Mr Harvey for undermining my ambitions, though I suppose he felt he was doing the right thing. I ran into him many years later and asked if he realised how much that decision had upset me. He was pretty frail by then, and he merely smiled and walked away without uttering a word.

The negative experience convinced me that I had to leave school that summer, in 1963, if I wanted to give football a real go. I was offered a trial for junior club Irvine Meadow, though I was still 15, and my first proper taste of playing with and against adult players was daunting. However it did not affect my form that much as I scored a hat-trick in a 4-1 win. When I tried to put on one of my shoes after the game, I found that a £10 note had been stuck inside. The Meadow manager urged me to say nothing and to treat it is as an indication that there could be more to come if I agreed to sign for them. But my sights were set on being fixed up with a senior club, so my heart soared when I was told that Bob Alexander, chief scout for Glasgow Rangers, had been present at the junior game. Now I'm not a Rangers fan, but the thought of getting a chance with one of Scotland's big two was enough to excite any lad. Joy soon turned to despair, however, when Bob visited us and revealed that the Ibrox club had decided not to sign me because they felt I was too small to make the grade at the top level. He added: 'We might come back in if you grow a bit over the next couple of years.'

I was devastated. It was as if my whole world had ended. I was convinced that my dream of becoming a professional footballer had been shattered, and I wondered if playing for Irvine Meadow might indeed be as high as I would gravitate. But all such fears evaporated on the Monday night after the junior game when there came a knock at the door of our home in Greenock. My parents answered, and the man standing in the doorway offered my mother a box of sweeties as a way of breaking the ice. He then said quietly: 'I want to sign your son Joe. I've seen him play school football many times, and believe he will go on to enjoy a wonderful career.' The man at the door was the legendary Hal Stewart, manager of Morton Football Club.

3

THE CAPPIELOW KID

*'Score a goal today, and I will get you a
new shirt with a proper collar'*

I shocked myself with my reaction when Hal Stewart came to
our home to offer me the chance to become a professional
footballer. I went close to turning him down, though for as
long as I could remember I had been dreaming of the day that I
would score a winning goal for Morton at Cappielow. For some
daft reason, I had it in my mind that Rangers might yet have a
change of heart and come back with an immediate offer instead
of waiting till I had come up with a miracle formula to make
myself taller. Hal said all the right things about how he had been
keeping an eye on me since hearing tales about the 'wee hardy
devil who can play a bit' who was showing promise in school
matches in Greenock. I had spoken often enough of how great it
would be for my pals at Mount School and Larkfield Boys' Club
to see one of their own turning out for the Morton first team, so
when I look back I cannot believe that I did not agree right away
to sign for Morton. Hal, to his credit, gave me time to think
things over . . . and my father soon put me right by reasoning:
'What's the point of holding out for an offer from Rangers that
might never come? Better to be a big fish in a little pond than the

other way around. If you do well for Morton, offers to go to bigger clubs will come.' I'm grateful that he intervened. I was 15, so I needed someone with wisdom to guide me. It's not that I didn't rate Morton, for I will remain an ardent fan until the day I die, but like many teenagers I was probably over-confident and convinced that I should be swept along in the fast lane to fame and fortune.

As it turned out, going to Morton was the best thing that could have happened, and Hal became like a second father in many ways. He nurtured my career and made sure that I was ready for the step up when it came. If I had gone to Rangers, I might well have been lost in the crush of kids hoping in vain for the chance to shine at Ibrox, and I might have slipped back into junior football. Hal told me from day one that he was sure I was good enough virtually to go straight into the Morton first team.

I must point out that he reflected a fairly laid-back style of management. In the 1960s football was fast heading towards the days when the manager supervised the training and could be seen shouting instructions from the dug-out, but not once did I observe Hal kitted out in a tracksuit or ordering proceedings on a training pitch. That said, there was no doubt that he ruled the roost at Morton, and the best compliment that I can pay him is to say that Hal was half a shrewd football manager and half an entrepreneur. He was decades ahead of his time when it came to marketing Morton and spotting potential to make money for the club. His methodology, thanks to having an eye for talent, was taking players to Cappielow for next to nothing, then selling them on for a healthy profit, and he was the first football figure in Britain to spot the value of raiding Scandinavia for players. Hal was highly popular with everyone at the club because he treated them with respect and fairness, but obviously his main aim was to see Morton win their matches. That was highlighted in novel fashion early in my career when we were due to face

Celtic at Cappielow, and Hal was struggling to raise a team because of a spate of injuries. The sun had been beating down in the west of Scotland, so Celtic officials must have been baffled when Hal made contact to inform them that he had called for the referee to inspect the pitch at Cappielow – because it was waterlogged.

I will not forget that day because when I arrived at the ground in the morning to help to prepare the kits for the game, I panicked slightly when I spotted a fire engine parked outside. I was even more perplexed to see that hoses were pumping water straight onto the pitch. They were left full on for several hours, with the result that the turf was under water in some places.

When the referee finally arrived, he expressed dismay that Greenock seemed to have been hit so badly by the weather while the citizens in nearby Glasgow were basking in sunshine. 'It must have been a freak storm,' I heard Hal inform the referee. 'So freak that the terraces have remained bone dry, I see,' replied the official, who made no further comment except to order the game to be played. Hal was forced to draft me in with a couple of other younger players, and he emphasised the need for us to keep the ball in the air as much as we could. 'Is that because of the state of the pitch?' I asked nervously, bearing in mind that I was but a rookie in that dressing-room. 'No,' Hal retorted. 'It's to make sure Celtic can't get it.'

Comments such as that endeared Hal to those who had the good fortune to play for him, and my affection for him shot sky-high when he handed me my first-team debut on Saturday, 9 May 1964. I was just 16. Morton were bound for Firhill to play Partick Thistle in the now-defunct Summer Cup. I was not initially included in Hal's squad, so I chose to travel to the match by train with other apprentice players. Because we were not meant to play, we grabbed the chance to stop off at a café for mince and tatties, and even dithered about doing a bit of shopping. We finally arrived at the ground at about 2.20 p.m., but the doorman at Firhill would not let us in because we were not wearing the club shirts and ties. He ordered us to pay at the boys' gate, and point-blank refused to believe that we were Morton players. He eventually relented when I retrieved my club tie from my pocket, and when I was let in I found out that Hal had been trying to track me down since about noon, because another senior player had been ruled out because of injury.

I cannot properly describe how excited I was when Hal told me that I would be on from the start, but the feeling almost changed to panic when he inquired: 'You are okay to play, aren't you?' I was terrified someone would tell him that not so long ago I had consumed enough food to keep half a team happy. 'Not a problem, gaffer,' I replied despite being in a sweat worrying that a bellyful of mince might make my first game in a Morton shirt a bit of a disaster. Given the lateness of my call-up, I didn't even have my boots with me, so I borrowed a pair from one of the Partick Thistle lads. Heaven knows what he thought when I utilised his footwear to score the only goal of the game!

As you would expect, I can still picture that debut goal in my mind. It came in the 38th minute after Morton had been awarded a free-kick. Kai Johansen played it forward low for Joe Caven to flick the ball on, leaving me with the easy task of slotting it past Jags' goalkeeper George Niven from around the penalty-spot. The crowd totalled an amazing 15,000 – the Summer Cup was a hugely popular competition – but the roar seemed as if it came from 100,000 throats as I celebrated. To be honest, the rest of the match is a bit of a blur, though I do recall feeling absolutely shattered at the end. Words of praise emanating from Hal soon perked me up, like music to my ears.

It was typical of Hal Stewart, who was a constant source of encouragement and who liked to lay down challenges to players in an effort to get more out of them. I can recall him making clear that he did not favour the style of shirt I wore, the sort with pins through the collar fashionable in the 1960s. 'Score a goal today, and I will get you a new shirt with a proper collar,' he promised; Hal also served as a director of the Co-op, so he had access to the best gear in their clothing department. I actually landed a hat-trick, and as he congratulated me after the match, he said: 'We'll make that three shirts then, shall we?' At the end of the next training session, he duly presented me with a trio of brand-new shirts, but there came a twist to the shirt tale. When I examined my wage packet that week, I noticed that the bonus I had received for the win was a lot less than the other lads were handed. Hal had deducted the cost of the three shirts! When I questioned him, he pointed out that he had offered to 'get' me three new shirts, and had not at any time mentioned that he would actually buy them. I didn't mind. I loved Hal, and I appreciated all that he did for me during my two spells at Morton.

I must say, too, that I was fortunate that Cappielow was almost bursting at the seams with football talent when I arrived keen as mustard, but as raw as a newly-cut steak. It's unlikely that I would have been able to make an impact at such an early age without the help of those players. As a striker, the one I looked up to most was another Cappielow legend, Allan McGraw, and I'm glad to say that he remains a close friend. During my first season with Morton, Allan set a British scoring record by netting an astonishing 58 goals in all competitions for the club. He was a hero to all the kids in Greenock, so it was a thrill to have the chance to train with him every day and to learn from one of the best strikers in the business.

Given his status, Allan could have given me the brush-off, as many senior professionals do when they are pestered by young-sters, but Allan is known as one of the true gentlemen of football for a reason. You will not find a nicer, more helpful individual in a game that can be cut-throat at times. Allan obviously detected my ambition to fill his place in the Morton team some day, but he was still happy to take time to present a personal master-class on how to get the better of defenders. He showed me how to hold the ball up and lay it off to bring team-mates into play. He also offered a handy tip on how to compensate for the lack of height that Rangers had been quick to highlight: 'Hitch a lift on the centre-half when you go for high balls.' According to Allan, it was all about timing your jump correctly to use the momentum of your opponent to help you get above him to meet the ball first. I spent a lot of hours working with him to perfect the technique, and the worthwhile advice meant that I was able to hold my own against some great centre-backs, including Celtic great Billy McNeill, who would normally have had no problems against a striker of my stature, standing all of 5ft 6in.

Allan McGraw's scoring exploits soon earned him a move to Hibs, so I had the chance to play alongside him only on a couple of occasions. Notice I said alongside him, for there was no hope of being picked instead of Allan. I was stuck on the wing and ordered to supply the crosses, from which he would score. I cherished those appearances, though, just as I cherish the fact that I'm now able to call Allan a friend. He is adored in Greenock because he served Morton for a total of 36 years as player, coach and manager. He rightly became known as Mr Morton for helping to win the old Scottish Second Division twice as player, then three lower-division titles as a manager. That was despite being left with a terrible legacy, because he was an unwitting guinea pig for the use of cortisone injections in his playing days. All Allan ever wanted to do was play, so when he was advised that taking those injections would help to mask any pain that he was feeling in his injured knees, he accepted the treatment. He had no idea that he was doing irreparable damage, and sadly is now in constant pain because of his shattered knees.

No one realised then that he was cutting his playing career short, and ensuring a lifetime of agony and discomfort in the process. Allan takes it all in his stride, so to speak, with lashings of good humour, and playing golf with him can be an unusual experience because his knees have a habit of slipping out of their joints without warning. One minute he will be lining up to strike the ball, the next he is collapsing in a heap because his legs have folded beneath him. His loyal pal Eddie Morrison is usually on hand to help to 'click' the knees back into place. It's not a pleasant spectator sport, but Allan will brush himself down and carry on playing as if nothing had happened. I have not met anyone who has a bad word to say about Allan, and I don't believe that he has ever told a lie. And he has always made himself available when I have needed to look to someone for advice and support.

It angered me when Allan was finally forced out of Morton in 1997 after the club fell into the hands of property developer Hugh Scott. Allan had taken me back to Cappielow as commercial manager at the time, so I knew how much hate had built up in the Greenock area for Scott, who had threatened to shut the club down and to build a supermarket on the Cappielow site. Outrageous! Allan would have none of that, and eventually helped a consortium of fans to force Scott out and to save the club. I know that pleased him greatly. It certainly pleased me.

Neither of us had any idea of what lay ahead back in 1963, when I was the wee chubby apprentice who cleaned Allan McGraw's boots and was inspired by his every word. I was also fortunate that other leading players at the club were only too happy to offer advice. Bobby Evans, the former Celtic star, was coming towards the end of his career, but he was still an outstanding performer for Morton. His sheer professionalism rubbed off on everyone, and he was particularly helpful to me when we took part in full games in training. They were usually straight contests between the first team and the reserves, and given how good Bobby was, I doubt that a raw 15-year-old would have got too many kicks of the ball in a head-to-head. 'Don't worry Joe, I will go easy on you,' Bobby would say. 'I will hold off a bit and give you a chance to do well, allow you a bit of time to improve your first touch.' I really appreciated that, because I'm convinced that Bobby's generosity had a lot to do with Hal giving me a chance so early in my Morton career.

We also had the services of John Little, a former Rangers player, at full-back. John, who was a schoolteacher as well as a footballer, was a lovely man, though he could annoy people at times because he was a bit fussy and set in his ways. He was into his 30s by then, but still shared digs in Gourock with Jim Smart and Billy Sinclair, who were apprentices with me and became close pals. I recall being at the digs and winding up John big style. He was out but had laid his pyjamas, neatly folded, on top of his pillow, as always, for when he returned, so we decided it would be fun to wrap them around the light hanging from the bedroom ceiling. Now we knew that John was too nice a person to switch on the light and risk waking the three of us when he got back, and we had to stifle our laughter as he stumbled about in the dark trying to trace his night attire. John had no problem spotting his pyjamas come the morning, and he did see the funny side of our larking about.

The club captain at the time was Jim Reilly, who had come to Morton from Third Lanark and was great at motivating everyone when the going got tough. Midfielder Morris Stevenson was one of the most underrated players I had the pleasure to line up alongside. He was the man who made all the passes, because he had great skill and a highly-developed football brain. He made Morton tick. I also received much help from that man of many clubs Jimmy Wilson, who was on the wing in my debut match against Partick. Aberdeen are among the clubs Jimmy signed for, and I'm glad to say that we now see each other on a regular basis at Pittodrie. Jimmy was a typical small, old-fashioned Scottish wide player, who did not receive the recognition that he deserved. Joe Caven, Eric Smith, Jimmy Mallen and Donnie McIntyre were among other players who did their bit to make sure I got on at Cappielow, and Hal had also gathered together a formidable coaching team, who included ex-Motherwell player Bobby Howitt and Doug Cowie, who was a notable performer with Dundee United.

The character we had to look out for was John Ellis, who was first-team coach and physio and weighed in at 20 stone-plus. John was the big joker in the pack, always making mischief such as putting salt in the tea or causing discomfort to many a player by rubbing Deep Heat on the skin side of jockstraps before the essential masculine supports were laid out among the kit on match days. Most of the apprentices, myself included, were taken in by one of John's favourite tricks . . . One of his jobs was to ensure that new kids saved the club money by clearing rubbish from the terracing after games, which few of us fancied. John stimulated a bit of enthusiasm by emptying his pockets to show us all the coins and other goodies, including a watch, that he claimed to have found when he helped to clear the terraces the last time. 'Anything you find you can keep,' he told us. We came across nothing of value, of course, and we would smile knowingly when we spotted John using the deception on the next batch of arrivals.

I did get my own back. I had scored a goal against Hibs at Cappielow, then made a point of running to celebrate at the corner furthest from the dug-outs. I was engulfed by delighted team-mates, and when they retreated I was left lying on the turf not moving a muscle. That prompted John to spring into action, and I could hardly contain myself as I watched out of the corner of my eye his huffing and puffing as he hauled 20 stones plus medical bag across the pitch as fast as he could. When John finally reached me, I feared he might have a heart attack as he panted: 'What's up, wee man?' I rolled onto my back, smiled and replied: 'Nothing . . . but what did you think of that goal?' In the interests of decency, I cannot reveal John's response as I got up and sprinted back to the half-way line to get the game restarted.

To add to our home-grown talent, we benefited from Scandinavian imports headed by Danish international goalkeeper Erik Sorensen. Hal's decision to become a trailblazer by taking in foreigners decades before it became commonplace was sparked by Morton's friendly against Copenhagen side Brønshøj Boldklub in the early part of 1964. He discovered that all the Danish players were amateurs, which meant that they could be snapped up for nothing. Erik was joined at Cappielow by Kai Johansen, Preben Artentoft and Borge Thorup as the Danish invasion gathered momentum, and it eventually reached the stage that six Danes were included in the Morton XI who played against Hearts in 1966. Denmark's loss was definitely Joe Harper's gain.

In those days most Scottish players tended to report for training for a couple of hours in the morning, then spend the rest of the day playing golf or snooker or making some bookmaker rich. So you can understand the fuss the Danes caused when they chose to spend their spare time heading back to Cappielow for even more training. I was still a kid and there was little else to keep me occupied in Greenock, so I asked Erik if it would be okay for me to join in. The sessions proved invaluable. They were fairly simple, involving us taking it in turns to meet crosses from either wing, then trying to volley or head them past Erik in goal. The Danes encouraged me to use the sessions to strengthen weaker points in my game, and my heading and ability to use the left foot improved considerably.

I doubt if I would have scored so many goals at the top level if I had not been party to skill-training from that wonderful group of Danish footballers. The sessions were also fun, particularly because Erik fancied himself as a bit of a striker. I lost count of the number of times that he lost bets when we switched positions, and he had a go at trying to get headers and volleys past me in goal.

With so many people apparently eager to help me, it was little surprise that I managed a few more first-team appearances after I had made my debut in the Firhill game. Hal persisted in playing me on the left wing to start with, mainly because those sessions with the Danes had made me more confident to have a go with my left foot. I managed to score seven goals the following season, despite still not fulfilling the role of first-team regular. Still, I was firmly established by the start of the 1966-67 campaign, and became the highest-scoring winger in the old Scottish Second Division with 27 goals. One of the highlights was helping Morton to reach the quarter-finals of the League Cup, a notable achievement for a lower-division club. We were drawn against Aberdeen when quarter-finals were played over two legs. We outplayed the Dons at Cappielow and won 3-1, and it should have been a lot more, but our dreams of making the Hampden final were dashed in heartbreaking fashion at Pittodrie. We were 3-2 up on aggregate until Jinky Smith made it 3-3 with five minutes to go. Aberdeen's Danish international Jens Petersen, who later became a great friend from our time together in the Granite City, netted the winner in the last minute. It was a sickener, but as the campaign neared its end, I was confident that my goals tally would be enough to convince Hal that it was time to give me a run in my more natural role as a striker. I was unaware that my days at Cappielow were numbered.

In March 1967 Huddersfield Town came in with a £45,000 offer, which constituted a massive bid for a novice professional finding his feet in Scotland's lower league. There was no way that Hal Stewart would turn it down, so that summer I found myself embarking on what I hoped would be a great adventure south of the Border.

4

Frustration in Fartown

'We received a voucher each day that entitled
us to a chip butty and a cup of tea'

To say that I hated every second of my time with Huddersfield
Town would be an understatement. The chances of my coming
to like the place evaporated when my grandfather Joe died after
a long battle against cancer.

I asked Huddersfield manager Tom Johnston and Ian
Greaves, the first-team coach, for permission to return to Greenock for the funeral. Greaves, who had been a top player with
Manchester United, surprised and disappointed me with his
reaction in backing up Johnston's orders that I should stay in
England, and not attend the funeral. Worse, I was warned that I
would be heavily fined if I went against their wishes. 'It's not as if
it's a close relative,' he maintained, the words convincing me at
that moment that I had to get out of Huddersfield. I remember
sitting tearfully back at the digs the club had organised for me,
and I was so upset that I contemplated packing in football
altogether. Grandad Joe was the man who had given me loads
of advice that had helped me to make it as far as Huddersfield in
the first place, and refusal of permission to pay my last respects
was yet another bad episode in what had proved a nightmare

experience. The only thing that stopped me walking out was the fear that it might upset my parents, who were coping with the loss of Grandad Joe. I also knew that it had meant a lot to my Grandad that I had done well enough to earn a move to England. So for the sake of his memory, I chose to stick it out for a while longer, but my heart was never in it despite the fact that Huddersfield were a decent side and their fans were supportive.

I confess that I was not exactly ecstatic when Morton boss Hal Stewart confirmed that he had agreed to sell me to Huddersfield for £45,000. For a start, I did not know where the place was, and the only time I had noticed the name was when I looked at the list of English football results in the *Evening Times Pink* on Saturday nights. It was a chance to make the first rung of the ladder in the English game, though, so I took the plunge.

When I finally found Huddersfield, I was hardly impressed to discover a rather grimy, unforgiving industrial town in Yorkshire, but I perked up a little when it was confirmed that my signing had been greeted well by the club's followers. The local papers described me as the 'new Denis Law', and journalists predicted that I would do as well as the Scotland legend had when he had taken the winding road southwards from Aberdeen as a teenager. I did feel confident, for I had just enjoyed a successful season that had seen me score 28 times for Morton, Sad to say it did not prove to be the case: I made 21 starts and scored three goals for Huddersfield Town, which is not how I had imagined my career working out.

I reckon that the way the club treated me from the start had much to do with my lack of momentum. For reasons best known to them, the club arranged digs in a district called Fartown, and if anyone mentions that place to me to this day, one word comes immediately to mind: s***hole. So far as I am concerned,

Fartown constitutes the backside of the universe, and if you are seeking instant depression, I would suggest booking a fortnight there. I must say that I don't know what it's like now, and certainly don't care to find out, but back in the 1960s it was a horrible place. You would imagine that the people at the club knew what Fartown was like, yet they chose the place to put up a young lad getting his first taste of life outside Scotland.

Living in Fartown was bad enough, but the accommodation only added to my gloom. It was not what I had expected when I agreed to move to England, for I was confined to a small attic which had six beds crammed in, and there was no room to swing anything, never mind a cat. Most of the occupants were Irish builders' labourers, who played as hard as they worked. They arrived back at all hours of the night after heavy drinking sessions, and it was almost impossible to get any rest. I don't blame my room-mates, for they were entitled to enjoy themselves because they grafted throughout the week, but it was tough on me, because clubs such as Huddersfield did not take players away overnight for matches. It was often the case that I found myself wide awake from 4 a.m. before a game on Saturday, because some of my room-mates had just made it back to the attic or they were so drunk that their snoring was threatening to peel off what served for wallpaper. Coping with that on a regular basis really began to get me down. The digs were directly across the road from St John's Stadium, home to Huddersfield Rugby League FC, so I eased my boredom and frustration by watching them train at night – anything to get me away from my attic situated in hell. I became friendly with a Dutch lad who played for the rugby club, but he was soon transferred, so I was left to soldier on, feeling lonelier with each passing day.

My only genuine salvation was playing for Huddersfield on Saturdays. That was because, thanks to Mr Greaves, I had come to hate training.

I was told that Greaves, who went on to manage Huddersfield after I had departed, had been a member of a special unit in the army in his younger days, and that came through on the training pitch. It is well documented that I was not the most enthusiastic of trainers later in my career; in contrast, at Huddersfield I was young and eager to impress, but some of the demands that Greaves made were beyond belief. His motto seemed to be the more he ran you into the ground, the better a footballer you would turn out. We were sent on regular, gruelling 10-mile runs, often with the famous Derek Ibbotson as our pacemaker. Derek was one of the best distance runners of his generation, an Olympic medallist who set a world record for the mile in 1957, and I have nothing against a gritty Huddersfield hero who was made an MBE in 2008 for services to athletics. He was certainly the best man to have in place to lead our races, but I would have defied even the best of athletes to keep up with him in those days. Most footballers certainly are not up to the task, and one or two of the more senior Huddersfield players were fined for jumping onto a lorry to take a lift back from one run. I *was* keen to make a good impression, but I have always wondered why on earth coaches like Greaves believed pounding the streets and countryside for miles on end would help to make better *footballers*. The runs that they make in games tend to be short, sharp bursts.

I was to discover later in my career, when I teamed up with Eddie Turnbull at Aberdeen, that players will work a lot harder if you throw a football into the mix at training sessions. My most painful memory of Greaves was formed after I had suffered damage to medial ligaments in a knee during a game. He saw me limping, and decided that he had the perfect way to get me fit again by using a heavy medicine ball – and making me go into 50-50 challenges for it with Trevor Cherry, the future England player. I was ordered to lunge into each tackle leading with my injured leg, and it was sheer agony. The more I cried out in pain, the more Greaves forced Trevor and me to carry on making the tackles. I'm no medical expert, but I could tell that was not ideal treatment for a player with an injury. And Huddersfield's idea of nutrition for players would have the army of dietitians now employed by clubs tearing their hair out. We received a voucher each day that entitled us to a chip butty and a cup of tea at a café near the stadium. I was fortunate that the meals served at my digs were designed to ensure that my Irish pals were prepared for a day's graft. The fare was basic but hearty, and it compensated for the fact that the only other hot food I tasted all day was that bread roll with its filling of soggy chips, which had to be smothered in ketchup to make them edible. Visits to the café did offer a small bonus in entertainment value because the red-checked tablecloth made an improvised draughts board. We would play for small change that we had gathered, and if a player's luck was in, he might have accumulated enough cash to purchase a decent meal at the weekend

I did get on reasonably well with the manager, at least until the death of my grandfather. Tom Johnston was a Scot who was born in Coldstream, and he was similar to Hal Stewart in many aspects of his approach. He did not wear a tracksuit, but was adept at encouraging players and offered lots of good advice. I had no problems playing for him, but the clouds of depression in which I was engulfed departed only when I was present in the dressing-room. What a dressing-room it was! Huddersfield had some marvellous players, and it gives me delight to be able to say that my eventual strike partner was Frank Worthington, one of the most skilful and colourful characters to feature in the English game. Frank was a rookie like me, but we made a great combination: his skill on the ball was amazing, and it was a real thrill to watch him at work. He had already begun to build his reputation as one of football's most flamboyant figures by sporting ankle-length leather coats and embracing an almost hippy-style, laid-back attitude to life.

I relished the nights that Frank invited me to join him for a few beers, and once we went for a weekend in Blackpool, where I experienced my second brush with the law, to add to the £1 fine imposed for trying to sneak into Cappielow as a boy. Frank swung an invitation with some ladies to a party at Pontin's holiday camp, which seemed more like a penal institution than a place to enjoy a vacation in the 1960s, for a strict curfew dictated that no-one would be allowed in or out after 7 p.m. Our party hosts had sneaked us in before the deadline and we had great fun, until it came to about 1 a.m. and we discovered that we had to find a way out. Frank came up with a master-plan, which involved running like mad towards the perimeter wall and simply scrambling over before security guards could catch us. We managed to make the top of the wall, but when we peered over the other side we noted that policemen were waiting to receive us. At this critical point, Frank and I were grateful that one of our team-mates at Huddersfield was Derek Parkin, whose career also saw him play for Wolverhampton Wanderers and England. 'You're Frank Worthington of Huddersfield aren't you?' one of the police officers inquired. 'Aye,' replied my bemused colleague. The policeman continued: 'You know Derek Parkin then? He's my cousin!' The constabulary had been accusing us of breaking into Pontin's bent on theft, but Derek Parkin's cousin came to our aid, cleared matters with his colleagues, and we were let off with little more than a reprimand.

Though Trevor Cherry, one of the most gifted England mid-field players, was at Huddersfield, the best player on the books for me was a defender named Billy Legg, who was rock-solid and so gifted that it was clear he had the potential to become a star at one of the major clubs and an England regular to boot. Billy's playing career was cut short, unfortunately, after he was seriously injured in a car crash a couple of years later, though he went on to make a worthwhile living as a coach. Another individual touched by tragedy was Jimmy Nicholson, formerly of Manchester United. But for a playing injury, he would have been among Matt Busby's squad who were involved in the Munich air disaster in 1958, and the man who took his place was killed in the tragedy. I don't believe that he coped fully with the aftermath of that most emotional of experiences, but Jimmy was still a fine player, and a real help to the younger lads at Huddersfield. Veteran of our squad was Mick Meagan, a Republic of Ireland international, who went out of his way to offer appropriate advice to a squad who were mostly on the young side. Winger Brian Hill, Chris Cattlin and Colin Dobson were there too, and mixing with them and learning from their example made those training sessions under Greaves at least bearable.

I confess that I came to dread the end of each working day at Huddersfield, when the lads went their separate ways, and in retrospect I realise that I should have merely packed my bags, headed home to Scotland and faced the consequences. I did not wish to let people down, though, particularly my parents, who may have taken it as a sign that I had failed. They would have supported me 100 per cent if I had baled out, but I chose to battle on because I was convinced that my determination to get to the very top in football would help me to cope. It was a desperately lonely existence, nonetheless.

The situation in Huddersfield improved considerably when I finally became friendly with Dave Marriot. First, let me say that I feel within my rights to observe that Huddersfield FC are partly to blame for the nation's bookmakers making a small fortune thanks to my investments over the years. Like many lads from

Greenock, I was interested in betting on horse-racing and other sports, but it developed into a vice at Huddersfield because sheer boredom led me to spend lots of time in the bookie's shop near my uninviting accommodation. Like most punters, I enjoyed only limited success – I've yet to meet a bookie who is poor – but the pain in my pocket was eased somewhat because Dave happened to be the manager of that bookie's office. We eventually became great friends and socialised regularly, and I acted as best man at his wedding.

On the subject of betting, in later years I gained a reputation for being a major gambler, which baffles me because the biggest single bet I ever placed was £100 and my largest win amounted to £4,500, which came thanks to an £11 stake on four horse-races. I don't consider that to be in the extravagant league, and it pales into insignificance when you consider the reported losses of today's leading players such as Wayne Rooney and Michael Owen. They have apparently said goodbye to hundreds of thousands of pounds, but after training in the 1970s my visits to the bookie involved bets of a few pounds at most. Team-mates would also lay wagers for fun, on who would score most goals in the season and such like, and I'm pleased to reveal that I came out on top on a few occasions. At Everton some players would act as bookmakers at team hotels with bets never more than £20, and the temporary bookies lost out from time to time, but it was just done for fun. No wonder I have to smile when it is suggested that Joe Harper lost all his money gambling, though I do indulge in a flutter on the horses to this day, and one 'betting' incident which I shall describe later did cause me angst

The parents of my bookmaker pal Dave Marriot were good to me too, and ended my digs hell by offering me Dave's room after

his marriage. I was most grateful for the use of that room and the kindness shown to me by them during the last few weeks of my Huddersfield career, but I had had quite enough of that football club. The only solution I could think of was to phone Hal Stewart to ask if he would take me back to Morton. Hal was most sympathetic as I listed the conditions that had contributed to my feeling desperately homesick. He chastised me for not calling him long before, and ended the conversation with a spirit-lifting: 'Leave it with me. I will see what I can do.' Things happened quickly, and my 18 months of torture at Huddersfield ended when I returned to Cappielow in August 1968 in a £20,000 deal. It meant a healthy £25,000 profit for Hal, which would have pleased him, but I knew too that it would not be long before he would be trying to sell me on again. I was just happy to be back at Morton, and near to my parents. Hal kept saying that I had simply gone to the wrong club, and he advised me to concentrate on doing my best for Morton, promising that if another team wanted me to join them, he would not let me go unless he was convinced that the move would be to my benefit.

During my absence, Morton had managed to qualify for the Inter-Cities Fairs Cup, which evolved into the UEFA Cup. It was rewarding to compete in the only European campaign for which my local club have qualified (so far) and even better that we were drawn against English giants Chelsea who boasted a host of notables in their ranks including Peter Osgood, Eddie McCreadie, Ron 'Chopper' Harris and England's international goalkeeper, Peter Bonetti. I was particularly excited by the prospect of appearing on the very pitch that Charlie Cooke had graced, having always admired the highly-talented Scottish international. The first leg was scheduled for Stamford Bridge for 18 September 1968, and we were hammered. Chelsea were magnificent in winning 5-0 with some breathtaking passing football, and I would have been as well paying to spectate for all the times that I touched the ball. Having read up on Harris and his reputation for kicking anything that moved, I was wary of facing up to him because Hal was still playing me out on the wing, but the home side's easy victory meant that 'Chopper' had no need to offer me examples of his distinctive talents.

Losing the match in London was bad enough, but the knowledge that some of my team-mates had taken drugs in an attempt to improve their performances made it even harder to handle. In those days it was common for players in England to pop pep pills, which were no more than glorified concoctions of vitamins, to give themselves a lift before games. They were pretty harmless and could hardly be described as hard drugs, and clubs in England openly allowed their use. But to my knowledge they were not used in Scotland, and I had certainly not set eyes on them until Morton trainer Eric Smith came into our dressing-room at Stamford Bridge to ask if any of us would like to try some. He did not offer them to anyone again, and I can only imagine that someone at Chelsea had told Eric that the potions might help us on our big European debut. I refused, but I believe one or two of the lads did take some pills, and the score-line suggests that they did not help our cause. No pills were in sight when we welcomed Chelsea to Cappielow for the second leg, in front of a bumper crowd of 25,000. The tie was over as such, but we made a fight of it and lost only 4-3 on the night. It was pleasing that we put on a good show on what was one of the biggest football events staged in Greenock.

❖

I was soon scoring regularly again in domestic football, including the only goal in a home league win over Aberdeen in November. Some rumblings could be detected about the Dons being keen on me, but nothing came of such rumours at that time, so I got on with re-establishing my Morton career. I was delighted to mark up a hat-trick within a 10-minute time-span to deliver a 3-3 draw away to Partick Thistle, after we had been 3-0 down. I also recall hitting a screamer from 35 yards past big Peter McCloy, who was in Rangers' goals in our 2-1 win at Ibrox. I was not so chuffed at still being cast on the wing because Joe Mason was in top form as our main striker, but I was content to be part of an exciting Morton line-up.

Chances to go back down to England began to re-emerge. I turned down an offer of a trial with Oldham Athletic and an invitation to spend some time with Hull City. The Huddersfield experience had left me too wary to head for unfamiliar destinations, though Hal mentioned that some interest was being shown by Sheffield Wednesday. I might have been brave enough to risk moving there because the Owls are among the sleeping giants of the game, but nothing came of it.

I scored against Aberdeen again at Pittodrie in April, and though we lost 6-3, it was enough to stir more whispers that manager Eddie Turnbull was planning to mount a bid. Again nothing happened, so I concluded that the best policy was to continue making the best of my second chance with Morton. If the prospect of a big move came, fine; if not, I would be happy to push forward to become a hero among the Morton followers. That was until dreams of performing for a club that had a chance of winning trophies were intensified at the end of that first season back at Cappielow . . .

The fixture-list had landed us with the misfortune of being the first team to face Celtic after they had clinched the league title. The game was to be played at Celtic Park, and I was not happy when Hal suggested that we should form a guard of honour for the Celtic team as they emerged onto the pitch as champions. 'I'm not doing that,' I protested to the boss, but he emphasised that anyone who was intent on defying him simply would not be picked. I was not the only unhappy Morton representative as we applauded Celtic into their theatre of dreams, and to add to the humiliation we were left languishing in the wings as they posed beside a massive table that was creaking under the weight of trophies that had been gained in the season. I vowed there and then that I would lift those trophies some day, though I realised that the ultimate experience was unlikely to be fulfilled with Morton. The game, though, ended with Morton proving to be the real stars of the show because we won 4-2. Per Bartram scored three, I added the other, and it was satisfying that we managed to spoil Celtic's party, even a wee bit. Morton finished in 10th place in the old 18-team First Division, which put us ahead of Hibs and Aberdeen among others, so we had good reason to be pleased with our efforts that season.

I was still at Cappielow at the start of the 1969-70 campaign, and pleased to continue challenging for selection as the club's first-choice striker, though personal circumstances changed dramatically after our visit to Pittodrie in September 1969. We drew 2-2, and I earned most of the headlines because our goals came from free-kicks that I completed successfully. Those strikes finally prompted Aberdeen to make their move.

5

ABERDEEN AT LAST

'McGarr, McKay, Harper . . . office!'

Eddie Turnbull once punched me so hard in the face that I was left with a black eye and a raging headache. The man could be absolutely terrifying at times, but I still love him like a father, and feel blessed that fate conspired for our paths to cross twice during my football career, at Aberdeen and Hibernian. Eddie is the best football manager I played for, better even than the great Alex Ferguson, by a country mile. Eddie was years ahead of his time when it came to tactics and innovative training ideas, and I reckon he was the inventor of the 'hairdryer' treatment that became Ferguson's trademark at Aberdeen and Manchester United. Eddie and I fell out on many occasions, but I would not swap the time I spent working under him.

I had obviously heard of Eddie Turnbull when Hal Stewart informed me that the Dons had finally made an official approach for my services. Eddie was one of Hibs' Famous Five, who thrilled Scottish football in the 1940s and 50s. I did not see him play, but I had heard all the tales about how talented and exciting he was with comrades Willie Ormond, Gordon Smith, Bobby Johnstone and Lawrie Reilly. All five scored 100 or more goals for Hibs, a remarkable achievement with a provincial club, and they helped them to win three league titles between 1948 and '52, historic proof that they were among the best players of their generation.

Hal summoned me to Cappielow, and I was bound for Glasgow's North British Hotel, where Eddie was waiting to speak to me. 'Don't think about it too hard,' Hal suggested. 'Unlike Huddersfield, this is a good move for you.'

While appreciating Hal's view, I decided that I simply had to speak to my father before doing anything else. I went straight from Cappielow to the shipyards, and the foreman was kind enough to call my father away from his workplace. 'The final decision is yours,' he told me. 'All I will say is I've read about Eddie Turnbull, and he seems like a good man.' That was enough to ensure that my mind was made up even before I met the imposing figure who was to do more for my football career than any other.

I was greeted at the hotel by Eddie and Bobby Calder, the noted Aberdeen chief scout who snatched many talented individuals from under the noses of the Old Firm, and persuaded them to head for the north-east of Scotland. Eddie explained that he was in the process of building a totally new team at Pittodrie after releasing 13 players because they had finished a lowly 15th in the league the previous season. He said just what I was desperate to hear: 'I want you to be my main striker, son,' and when he pointed out that Aberdeen were breaking their club transfer record by paying Morton £40,000 for me, I felt excited and honoured. I agreed a contract of £45 a week, generous wages at the time, and Eddie also included a £3,000 signing-on fee.

My contract was for three years, with a further three-year option if I did well, and what was not immediately apparent was that Eddie had got me to agree to be paid £45 a week for the next six years! The contract made no mention of pay rises if I was successful at Pittodrie, and remember that these were the days before players could call upon an army of agents and solicitors for independent advice. Eddie was experienced in these matters, and no doubt felt that he had completed a satisfactory bit of business for Aberdeen FC. None the wiser, I was happy to shake his hand, and prepared to make my way back to Greenock to tell my parents that I had made the big time at last. 'Where do you think you are going?' Eddie inquired. 'Home to get my kit packed,' I replied. 'Forget that – you have a game at the weekend to prepare for.' The manager handed Bobby and me tickets for the train to Aberdeen. I had no boots, no change of clothes, just the suit and shoes I was standing in, but who was I to argue?

After we arrived in the Granite City, I was met by my first sample of the Doric, the distinctive dialect that residents in the north-east adopt to bemuse visitors. When Bobby and I entered a taxi, the driver asked: 'Right loon, where do you want to go?' I thought the cabbie was implying that I was some sort of lunatic, and was so shocked that I was about to present the guy with a mouthful for being so rude to a stranger. Bobby intervened to point out that loon is the word used by Aberdonians to describe a young boy, and I spent the rest of the road journey wondering if I would need to find myself a translator as well as a new pair of football boots.

As I wandered about Pittodrie Stadium on my first day, I had a feeling that this was the start of something special. The day ended in a meeting with Derek McKay, who was to become my closest pal at Aberdeen. Sadly Derek died in April 2008 while I was in the process of writing this book.

I was on holiday in Las Vegas, USA, when news came

through that he had died suddenly aged just 59, while enjoying a break in Thailand with his stepson. I shed tears. Derek was best man when I married Fiona in July 1972, and he made a controversial speech – going on about his delight that he would now have access to all the women I had left behind, though using slightly more basic terms – but I forgave him because I loved Derek to bits. He played only a handful of first-team games for the Dons and scored just four goals, but as I will reveal later, these were special goals. Derek left Pittodrie in 1971 and his career took him to South Africa, Hong Kong and Australia, where he eventually chose to settle in Perth. We always kept in touch, and I loved it when he made his all-too-infrequent visits home. The last was in 2005, when I organised a reunion for the Dons side who won the Scottish Cup in 1970. Derek was in Aberdeen for several weeks and my liver was screaming for mercy by the end of it all, because he loved a good night out. His untimely death means that I treasure even more those few weeks of laughter and recalling our good old days.

My first meeting with Derek took place at the Brentwood Hotel, Crown Street, Aberdeen, which the Dons had decided would serve as my digs. I walked into 'my' room to discover Derek lying on one of the beds. I had not realised that I was expected to share a room, and I was a bit wary, especially after my experiences enduring the company of Irish labourers at Huddersfield. I soon warmed to the idea, however, mainly because Derek was such a kind-hearted and friendly companion. I doubt that he did anyone a bad turn; he was generous with his time and money, and he believed that life was for living to the full. We developed a close friendship with Ian Broadley, a journalist from Dumbarton who had moved to Aberdeen to report on the Dons for the *Daily Record*. Ian covers the club, on a freelance basis, to this day. We enjoyed lots of fun, usually with

Derek leading the way around the pubs and dance halls of Aberdeen, particularly the Palace in Bridge Place. Derek and I got into some scrapes, mainly because of the presence of several older guys at Pittodrie, who were up for leading their fresh-faced team-mates astray. Chief among them was goalkeeper Ernie McGarr, who enjoyed a brief spell as Scotland's first choice while he was at Pittodrie, and a boozy day out with Ernie led to the black eye planted by Eddie Turnbull.

Heavy snow meant that our game at Pittodrie was postponed, and Eddie told us to take the rest of the Saturday off with the words: 'Go and have a bit of fun and relax.' Ernie, Derek and I took our manager's advice too literally, however, and ended up absolutely bladdered, so to speak. When we eventually emerged from the pub, we discovered that snow had continued to fall, and it was now so deep that roads were blocked and taxis and buses had been withdrawn from service. We spotted some workmen huddling around a glowing brazier in the Castlegate, a picturesque area at the top of Union Street, Aberdeen's main thoroughfare. Beside them was an old bus, which had been adapted to act as a snowplough, with a space on board for carrying sand, which was spread to ease driving and walking conditions. I recall Ernie asking the workmen if he knew of any way we could get home, and one of them, no doubt for a laugh, suggested that we take the adapted bus. Thus Ernie started to drive it down King Street, with Derek and I on the back shovelling sand out onto the pavement and cars as we proceeded.

Given the amount of drink we had consumed, it was a terrible thing to do and thankfully – despite the state we were in – we had travelled only 50 yards or so before we realised the error of our ways. Ernie switched the engine off, gave the keys back to the workmen, and we staggered off into the night to slip and slide our way through ever-deepening snow.

I thought the episode had passed without repercussions until Eddie Turnbull came in for training on the Monday and shouted: 'McGarr, McKay, Harper . . . office!' Ernie made the long walk down the corridor first, and we could hear the manager ranting and raving and telling him that his days as a Dons player were numbered for getting so drunk that he would risk such daft actions. I had not been at the club that long, and I admit that I was shaking as I attempted to lace my boots and prepare for training. Derek was next in for treatment, and as I peeked down the corridor I could see Ernie returning from the office white-faced and clearly shaken. 'I'm not going to get the sack, am I Ernie?' I blurted out, genuinely worried that I had blown my chances of becoming a star with Aberdeen. 'Not if you follow my lead,' replied Ernie. 'Eddie is a man's man. Just go down there and stand up for yourself. Show Eddie you won't be treated like a wee boy. He will respect you, and you will be fine.' When my turn came, I passed Derek in the corridor and he was even more ashen-faced than Ernie had been, and on entering Eddie's office I was greeted by a roar of: 'Sit down, you bastard!'

As ordered, novice Don Joe Harper sat down on the small seat in front of the manager's desk, and the gaffer started to lay into me. It took some guts, but I decided to take Ernie's advice and to make a stand in what I feared could be a last chance to salvage my Aberdeen career. 'Look here, boss,' I declared, though aware that Eddie's eyes were almost bulging out of his head with anger. 'I may be one of the younger players, but I'm not going to sit back and accept you talking to me like that, and treating me like a wee schoolboy. I want to be treated like a man.' That's when Eddie caught me with a right hook that would have done any top-class boxer proud. He caught me under the left eye, and sent me sprawling back in the chair, which then balanced precariously against the door behind. I was stunned, but still sufficiently conscious to realise that it would be sensible to shut up. Eddie was right in my face, spraying me with spittle as he dared me to utter another word of defiance. All I can recall from then was a sequence of 'Yes sir/No sir' as I readily agreed with everything the man was saying. I sheepishly made my way back to the dressing-room, staggering and with my left eye starting to swell so badly that I could hardly see. I was greeted by Ernie laughing uproariously with all the other lads, who had been briefed on the good advice that my supposed pal had offered. The manager gave all three of us another chance, but I had learned not to mess with him.

Derek and I still managed to enjoy ourselves, for we were almost joined at the hip, but we made sure that our leisure periods were as low-key as possible from then on. It's strange how we hit it off instantly, but Derek and I went everywhere together, including taking the bus from Union Street to Pittodrie for my first day of full training as an Aberdeen player. Can you imagine a professional footballer travelling to work with the punters on the bus these days? I might have been the club's record signing, but I could not afford the luxury of a car at that stage.

I might have been well-paid, but not to the unrealistic levels witnessed in football nowadays. The Pittodrie car park is often filled these days with fancy new wheels owned by youth players who might not even graduate to the first team, and I often wonder whether that is one of the main reasons why there is such a dearth of fine young players coming through. When I started, you had to work to be able to afford luxuries such as a car and fancy clothes. The Aberdeen players were all on the same basic wage, but the bonuses were generous if we won games. That helped to make our team spirit strong. It made us work that little bit harder, because we knew that if we lost it would result in less money coming in, and maybe a bit of hardship for those who were married with children. That hunger has vanished because younger players are spoiled, and they don't need to worry so much about bonuses.

❖

My main aim in October 1969 was to establish myself in the Aberdeen side. When I reported for work for the first time, I was given two pairs of brand-new boots, a novel experience coming from Morton, and Eddie's training was a revelation. He was my first tracksuit manager. All my previous bosses had tended to wear shirt and tie and to spend their days in the office.

Trainers took the training, and you encountered managers at team talks or on match days. Eddie was different. He was out there early every day setting up training, and he took part in many of the drills and exercises that he had organised. Training was never boring under Eddie. Many techniques that he introduced, such as games with limited numbers of players and ball-skills exercises, are now commonplace, but they provided a thrill for footballers in 1969, because we had been more used to long-distance running and sprints. I was told that before Eddie arrived at Aberdeen, the players were allowed to train using footballs on Fridays only. The theory was that this would make them more hungry for the ball during games on Saturdays. Under Eddie, footballs were in evidence on each and every day, and the emphasis was on improving skills and learning how tactics could change during matches.

To be sure, we still had to run around Aberdeen's winding Seaton Park or along the beachfront, especially as punishment if we had lost a game. I hated these sessions because I was never the best of long-distance runners, and I'm afraid tales of me hiding amid the bushes at Seaton Park to miss the odd lap or two, then rejoining the run to the finishing line, are quite true. Eddie confided years later that he always knew when I had gone missing, but he had said nothing because I gave my all in the rest of training and in games.

I loved working with Eddie, who taught me much about football, and it was clear that he knew the game inside out. That meant he always got the respect that he deserved from everyone at Pittodrie. The worst thing about him, though, was that he could be moody, and you never knew the best way to approach him on a day-to-day basis. I would greet him with a 'Good morning, boss', and if he responded with a 'Good morning', I knew that I would be able to joke and have a laugh during training. If he merely grunted and walked on, it was a case of keeping your head down, getting the work done and making sure that you did not give the boss an excuse for punishing you for a misdemeanor. I knew after those first few days of training under Eddie that I had made a move that would improve me as a player. The Dons were due to travel to Ayr United in what would be my debut game, and Eddie kindly allowed me to divert to Greenock on the Friday night to visit my parents, who had been a bit shocked that I had travelled directly to Aberdeen a few days earlier after heading into Glasgow simply to discuss the possibility of joining the club.

My parents have told me often that they had never seen me so excited. I hardly slept on Friday night because I was dreaming about starting my career as a Dons striker with a bang, by scoring the winner at Ayr the next day. I was disappointed when Eddie told me that I would be operating on the right wing, with former Rangers star Jim Forrest and big Davie Robb the men preferred to get forward in the more central striking positions. Even worse, an injury to Danish defender Henning Boel meant that I ended the game playing at right-back. Eddie had already used our substitute – only one was permitted then – so I had no choice.

I have often joked with Eddie that he invented the overlapping attacking full-back that day, and I spent most of the time left with the manager shouting and screaming at me to get back. Big Davie got our goals in a 2-1 victory, so it was pleasing to have made a winning start as an Aberdeen player. The Aberdeen *Evening Express* reported the following Monday that 'the new boy Harper had a serviceable start for the Dons, and looked as if he will fit in'.

The clash with Partick Thistle the following week, on 11 October 1969, is special because that was the occasion on which I claimed the first of my 205 goals for the Dons. It came from the penalty-spot in the 85th minute, and gave us a 2-1 success. It did not prove to be the most spectacular of starts by some standards, but I have always cherished the experience because it was the first of so many unforgettable Pittodrie days for me. I reckon it was my impromptu celebration after netting that spot-kick – I dropped to my knees behind the goal, raised my arms and bowed to the Dons fans – that led eventually to my being crowned King of the Beach End, which refers to the section of Pittodrie favoured by the most loyal members of the club's Red Army. The celebration had not been rehearsed and I had not performed it before, but it became my trademark. Sliding along on my knees watching all those delighted Aberdeen fans celebrating in unison was one of the biggest thrills of my life, and I still get a tingle down my spine thinking about it.

My theory is that the King nickname evolved from fans bowing back towards me, which you see often at games now, but I cannot recall that happening in Scotland before Dons followers embraced the habit in the 1970s.

❖

Aberdeen fans created a song for me, to the tune of *Just One of Those Songs (That You Hear Now and Then)* which was recorded by one of my favourite artists, Barbra Streisand, and a host of others. It went:

'Do you ken Joey Harper, the king of the north,
He plays at Pittodrie, just doon fae Kincorth,
He drinks all the whisky and Newcastle Brown,
King Joe Harper's in town.'

For those not familiar with all the words, *ken* means *know* and *Kincorth* is a district in the southern part of Aberdeen. Opposing fans, particularly those following Celtic, sang less kind songs. I recall when I was being carried off by stretcher after being injured at Celtic Park that their support started to chant:

'Roll out the barrel,
Harper's a barrel of sh***, sh***, sh***!'

The referee threatened to book me for the gesture that I made back from the stretcher, but I took this as good-natured banter, and it added to my enjoyment of games.

Going by the words that rang out, fans clearly thought I was a bit of a boozer, which was not exactly true. I was like any working man in enjoying a few pints with my mates, but did not allow strong drink to interfere with my ability to play football. As noted elsewhere, in bachelor days my main drinking buddies were Derek McKay and journalist Ian Broadley, and we did enjoy some wild times together. Drinking could be pretty heavy on Saturday and Sunday nights in Aberdeen's pubs and clubs, and Derek and I might enjoy the odd pint on a Monday or Tuesday, but Wednesday was the cut-off point for boozing.

Eddie Turnbull would not have countenanced our touching a drink in the lead-up to a game, and I was always in control of my drinking, unlike individuals such as Tony Adams and Paul McGrath in later years. It annoys me then that some people claim they used to see me out clubbing on a Friday before scoring a hat-trick for the Dons on a Saturday. Mere folklore. That never happened. I had too much respect for my club and profession to act in that way. I must add, however, that regular post-match drinking *was* part of the football culture in the 1970s, and it helped the team to bond and to make vital contact with our faithful fans. I think it is sad that modern professional footballers tend to be more aloof from the supporters who underpin their wages . . . Mixing with the fans was one of the best aspects of the job, so far as I was concerned.

Our league form in 1969-70 was inconsistent, not helped by the fact that Martin Buchan, our captain and star defender, missed much of the first part of the campaign because he was injured in a car crash. That led to the curious situation in which Bobby Clark, the club's long-term first-choice goalkeeper and a Scotland regular who had lost his place because Ernie McGarr was doing so well, played a couple of games at centre-back when the Dons lost at Rangers and St Johnstone. Ernie went on to claim Bobby's place in the Scotland side, which made Aberdeen the first provincial club to have the national No. 1 and back-up keepers in their squad at the same time.

Matters sorted themselves out, and Bobby was promoted to the rank of Dons legend, ending his career by helping the club to win the league in 1980. There was no chance of a league triumph in 1969, though, and the Dons had been knocked out of the Scottish League Cup in the quarter-finals by Celtic before I arrived. With our hopes of staying in touch with Celtic in the title race vanishing – they eventually took the championship by 12 points from Rangers with Aberdeen eighth, a further 23 points behind – the Scottish Cup was our best hope of making an impact. Aberdeen had not lifted that trophy since 1947, and had lost 2-0 to Celtic in the 1967 final. Eddie had been forced to miss that trip to Hampden with the Dons because he was ill, and the players claimed that cost them the cup.

When we were drawn against Clyde at home in the first round in January 1970, Eddie felt that we were good enough to make the final again if we applied ourselves properly. That was despite the fact that our poor league form had seen us go six matches without success in the lead-up to New Year.

I was under pressure because I had failed to score since netting the penalty winner against Partick, and if that was not sufficient to bear, I was injured in a car crash near Portlethen, south of Aberdeen, the day before we were due to meet Clyde. My face smashed against the windscreen, which shattered, and I was left with 42 stitches and so many cuts that my face looked like a road map. I had also suffered three cracked ribs and could hardly breathe, so I resigned myself to missing the chance to face the Bully Wee in the cup.

The gaffer was kind enough to include my name on the team-sheet, which was pinned on the noticeboard at Pittodrie, and I thought that he was just being nice and trying to keep me involved. I got the shock of my life when Eddie told me that I would be starting the game. I did not protest: I was a professional, and if the manager felt that I was still capable of doing a job despite my misfortune, I was willing to give it my best shot. It annoys me when I read nowadays of players withdrawing from games because of thigh strains and niggly knocks that we tended to cope with most weeks. Players were certainly made of sterner stuff in the 1970s!

I looked a bit like Frankenstein's monster when I went out to take on Clyde at Pittodrie, my face stitched up and ribs strapped tightly. My problems worsened within the first couple of minutes when one of my team-mates, perhaps big Henning Boel, sliced a pass aimed for me, and the ball battered me full in the face. I felt some of the stitches go and blood began to pour down my face, but it would be some time into the future before referees ordered a player to leave the pitch at the slightest hint of blood.

Clyde were struggling in the old First Division, eventually just escaping relegation, and they did not put up much resistance. Despite the gore and the sore ribs, I marked my Scottish Cup debut for the Dons with a goal after six minutes. I scored again in the 36th minute, and Davie Robb marked up a double as well as we strolled to a 4-0 victory.

Thoughts of Hampden glory almost evaporated in the second round, despite the fact we were drawn at home to Clydebank, one of the weakest sides in the Second Division. The tie was played on a Wednesday night because snow had forced a postponement the previous weekend, and we were simply dire and lucky to escape with a 2-1 victory thanks to goals by Jim Forrest and Davie Robb. The Dons fans, quite rightly, booed us off the pitch, and our form was so bad that our supporters had been urging Clydebank to grab an equaliser. The Dons have taken a lot of stick over the years for being shocked in cup-ties by the likes of Stenhousemuir, Queen's Park and Queen of the South, and we came close to being the victims of one of the biggest shocks of all, because losing to Clydebank at home would have been a major embarrassment. Eddie went ballistic in the dressing-room and told us we should be ashamed of the way that we had performed; he believed that we were lucky not to be lynched, never mind jeered, by our support. Thoughts of playing in the final were far from our minds as we sulked in the dressing-room that

February night, heads bowed and listening to Eddie rip into us. But fortunes were about to swing back dramatically in Aberdeen's favour . . . with my room-mate and best pal Derek McKay emerging as the unlikely hero of a cup run that older Aberdeen fans recall with delight.

6

THE ROCKY ROAD TO HAMPDEN

'The manager had been worried about my dip in form'

A football fairytale as magical as the one created at Aberdeen by my pal Derek McKay is unlikely to be repeated. The second half of the 1969-70 season would see him earn the nickname Cup-tie, and create a legend that will forever remain part of the Pittodrie folklore. Derek had been less fortunate than I had during the first few months of his Aberdeen career. Though born in the fishing village of Macduff, north-west of Aberdeen, he was originally overlooked by the Dons despite making his debut for Dever-onvale in the semi-professional Highland League when aged 15. He was eventually signed by Dundee, but struggled to achieve recognition at Dens Park, and he was surprised and delighted when Aberdeen employed him on a free transfer just prior to my arrival. Eddie Turnbull made it clear from the start that Derek would be little more than a squad player. Derek wanted more than that, so he kept playing away with the reserves while I was striving to establish myself in the first team.

After toiling to beat Second Division strugglers Clydebank on our own patch in the second round of the Scottish Cup, we were a bit worried when we were drawn in the quarter-finals away to Falkirk, who were chasing promotion from the same division.

Our last league match before the trip to Brockville resulted in a 1-0 home defeat by Airdrie, and we were again booed off the park by our irate fans. Drew Jarvie, who was soon to become a team-mate, scored the goal, and the reverse ended Ernie McGarr's short spell as our first-choice goalkeeper. A flu epidemic also meant that we had serious selection problems ahead of the cup-tie, but Derek admitted that he was still a bit surprised to be told by Eddie that he would start on the right wing at Brockville. 'Eddie said if I do well I will stay in the team,' he added.

Derek was outstanding, proving a handful for the opposing defenders throughout the game, and he grabbed the only goal in the 66th minute. True to his word, the manager kept Derek in the team for the semi-final clash with Kilmarnock at Muirton Park, Perth – now the site of a supermarket – and my mate delivered again, scoring the only goal after 21 minutes. A riot between the rival fans broke out at the end, and we were forced to dodge flying bottles and cans as we made our way up the tunnel.

We didn't care that much, for thanks to Derek's two goals we suddenly found ourselves preparing for a Scottish Cup final. 'I would like to see the boss drop me from the final now,' Derek observed as we discussed the victory over Kilmarnock while sipping a few pints back in Aberdeen. He was a certain starter for the showdown with Celtic at Hampden, but I was not so lucky. My own form and that of the first team in league fixtures had continued in patchy mode, so much so that Eddie dropped me to the reserves in the weeks before the final. I missed the shock 2-1 win over Celtic in Glasgow in March 1970, which had temporarily prevented Jock Stein's side from winning the league title. Celtic, curiously, actually provided Eddie with the ammunition needed to motivate the Dons at Hampden the following month. One of our lads mentioned to the gaffer that he had spotted Celtic officials carrying crates of champagne into their dressing-room in anticipation of celebrating another championship. Eddie went ballistic, and I was told that he delivered one of the most amazing and inspiring pre-match talks: the basic theme was that there was no way in which Aberdeen would reach the position where 'those bastards' were celebrating next door. 'Let's make them choke on that champagne,' Eddie concluded before shaking the hand of each player as they left the dressing-room.

The stirring words certainly worked on our young winger Arthur Graham, who had made his first-team debut as a substitute at the age of 17 in a 2-1 home win over Dunfermline the previous week. Eddie handed Arthur his first start against Celtic, who needed two points to guarantee that the champagne corks would be popping. Arthur certainly was not fazed by the enormity of the occasion, setting up the opening goal with a pass that George Murray slotted away. He then nodded home the second to cap one of the most remarkable first starts for any young lad at the Dons. Tommy Gemmell pulled a goal back for Celtic late on, but it was Arthur who hogged the headlines the next day. It was a pity I missed all the fun because I had been banished to the reserves, and the worry that I would not make selection for the cup final was at the forefront of my thoughts.

My hopes were raised a little when I was taken back in for the game with Dundee United the following week, but we lost 2-0 and Eddie clearly was not happy with the way I played. The next week, seven days before the final, I was packed off with the reserves again to play Hearts at Tynecastle, while the first team prepared for Hampden by facing the Jam Tarts in the league at Pittodrie. I was devastated because I was convinced Eddie was intent on leaving me out of the final, particularly when you recall that only one substitute could be named. If I fell short of making the first-team squad of 18 for a league game before the final, what chance of being one of the lucky dozen for the big occasion? When Hearts gave us a first-half battering in the reserve game – we were 3-0 down by half-time – I was even more certain that I would miss the biggest game of the season. Teddy Scott, a wonderful man who was trainer and coach of the reserve side and who helped to guide many careers at Aberdeen FC, took me aside in the Tynecastle dressing-room and confided that I would 'need to do something special' to make the cup-final squad. I went out and battled as if my life depended on it, completing a hat-trick to earn a 3-3 draw.

We had to face Kilmarnock at home in the league on the Monday, so I was extremely pleased that my exploits at Tyne-castle earned a recall to the starting line-up. We drew 2-2, but I felt I had played much better, and I almost felt like kissing old Teddy when he whispered to me at the end that the boss had decided I would definitely be starting at Hampden: I would be going out against Celtic determined to make the most of an opportunity that I feared I had blown. Eddie and Teddy told me years later that they had always intended to play me in the final. The manager had been worried about my dip in form, and he hoped that scoring a few goals for the reserves would help to boost my confidence. He also revealed that he had left me out of the league clash with Celtic because he feared that they would attempt to injure me, thus ruling me out of the final. 'Never underestimate how ruthless Jock Stein and that Celtic team were,' he said. I had little idea of what was going on in the background, but it was another example of Eddie's catalogue of managerial skills. He always seemed to know exactly what to do and when to do it, and how to inspire the right frame of mind in players preparing for big games.

We stayed in the imposing setting of Gleneagles Hotel the night before the final. At breakfast our goalie Bobby Clark ordered a glass of orange juice to accompany his cereal and toast, only for Eddie to come up and remove the drink. Bobby is one of football's true gentlemen, but he was not best pleased to be told what he could consume, or not, for breakfast. When he asked Eddie why he could not have the orange juice, the boss replied: 'Because I said so.' Bobby was like a bear with a sore head for the rest of the day, and he was still grousing about the orange juice incident during the pre-match warm-up. It was a tiny interlude amid life's trials and tribulations, but it ensured that one of our most experienced and important players was really fired up by the time the game started.

Celtic, who had by now clinched the league and beaten Leeds United in the first leg of their European Cup semi-final, were hot favourites to grasp the Scottish Cup. They were Hampden regulars. This would be their 26th appearance at the national stadium under Stein alone, while Aberdeen would be contesting their seventh final ever; their only triumph, remember, had come two years after the end of the Second World War. Celtic fans still claim that Aberdeen defied the odds only because referee Bobby Davidson went against their team, and helped us. Utter nonsense! We won because Eddie Turnbull had gradually built up a side with the right blend of youth and experience, and we all performed at our peaks on that wonderful afternoon of 11 April 1970. They were all wonderful characters in their own right.

Bobby Clark was one of the most talented goalkeepers of his generation. Eddie took him to Pittodrie from Queen's Park, and he gave the Dons outstanding service for more than 15 years. He was the club's most capped player until the successes of the 1980s allowed the likes of Jim Leighton, Willie Miller and Alex McLeish to overtake his tally. Bobby was by far the fittest and most dedicated professional I worked with, and he deserves credit for the part he and Lenny Taylor, a schoolteacher in Aberdeen in the late 1970s, played in modernising Aberdeen FC's youth-coaching system. They organised proper sessions for the best youngsters, and they helped to unearth future stars such as John Hewitt, Neale Cooper and Neil Simpson. They also travelled around schools in the Aberdeen area encouraging teachers to coach the children and spreading the word about the club. I can reveal that co-author Charlie Allan benefited from Bobby's trademark generosity after a coaching session in 1972, when he was a pupil at Harlaw Academy. Unfortunately for the fresh-faced Charlie, when he returned to the dressing-room he discovered that his trousers had been pinched in a break-in. The trousers were not that important, but a ticket for that evening's Aberdeen v Juventus UEFA cup-tie had been tucked in a pocket, and not surprisingly that had been spirited away too. The ever-helpful Bobby came to the rescue, driving Charlie home and returning an hour or so later with a replacement ticket for the big game. New trousers for the laddie could wait.

Bobby is now in the USA working as the head of football (soccer) coaching at Stanford University. He has given a lot more back to the sport than he took out of it, and I was delighted to see that the Dons welcomed his old pal Lenny back on board, as head of youth development, in 2005. Bobby was still chasing his first winners' medal in 1970.

Henning Boel, our big right-back, was a vastly underrated player who never performed better than on that day in Glasgow. He was so much on top of his game that Stein was forced to change his left-winger three times, and John Hughes, Jimmy Johnstone and finally Bertie Auld all tried, and failed, to get the better of our great Dane. Henning was one of the quieter men of our squad, mainly because it took him a fair bit of time to learn English. We would all laugh when Henning smiled broadly and said thanks in response to centre-half Tommy McMillan describing him as a 'dour big bastard' when he arrived every day for training. I was clear that Henning was convinced his teammate was being complimentary, though once he had mastered the language no more wind-ups emanated from Tommy.

Jim Hermiston, a left-back who possessed a dry sense of humour, was particularly adept at winding Eddie up. When he was warned that he would have to restrict the space in which Bobby Murdoch was given to operate, he kept asking the gaffer to point out exactly who that was. Murdoch was the star for Celtic at the time, so we were obliged to bite our tongues to stop ourselves laughing as Eddie provided Jim with a detailed description of his opponent. Jim was a courageous competitor who went on to captain the Dons before surprising everyone by quitting the club to become a policeman – because he would enjoy better pay and job security. Can you imagine a contemporary captain of Aberdeen having to make that life-changing decision?

It transpired that Jim was among the police officers who walked in front of the team's open-top bus when we paraded down Union Street after winning the Scottish League Cup in 1976. That must have been a weird experience for him. Later he displayed a different type of courage soon after he had retired from the police force in Australia, where he had chosen to settle with his family. Jim tackled an armed criminal who was attempting to rob a bank. During the tussle the culprit managed to aim the gun against Jim's head and pulled the trigger, but thankfully it failed to fire, though it was loaded. Jim received a bravery award for his efforts; he did not shirk a challenge during his football career either.

Big Tommy McMillan was at the heart of the defence alongside skipper Martin Buchan, who had recovered from injury problems. I maintain that Tommy did not receive the credit that he was due for his part in that successful spell for the Dons, after the years of under-achievement and struggling to stay in the First Division. I gave Tommy the nickname of Quiet Assassin because he was one of the toughest and most ruthless defenders that I encountered. He did not hesitate when it came to putting the boot in, but he tended to wander away from even the toughest of challenges, complete with a broad smile. Some opponents tried to get back at Tommy by clattering into him, but again he would just get back up, smile and get on with the game without uttering a word. That smile was an assurance for us that the poor bloke who had battered into our giant at the back would soon get his come-uppance.

Tommy was much more than a tough tackler, though. His partnership with Martin was one of the most solid and formidable in Aberdeen's history, and I would place it on a par with the one forged by Willie Miller and Alex McLeish in the 1980s. Tommy and Martin underlined that the following season by helping the Dons to achieve a British record of 12 league games without conceding a goal during a run of 15 successive victories. Martin was the perfect foil for Tommy, and we always felt we had a chance of winning games when they were paired at the back.

I was fortunate that my career included spells playing in front of Martin Buchan and Willie Miller, who were without doubt the most influential captains and talented defenders in the club's history. I have been asked many times which one was the better, but I tended to dodge a judgment because I have great respect for both, and did not wish to cause offence. I will answer the question now by saying that Martin just edged it in my view. Willie was the greatest Dons captain and club servant, and his haul of trophies during a 20-year playing career at Pittodrie proved that. He was also an excellent penalty-box defender and one of the fiercest competitors on a football pitch. Martin reflected the same winning mentality as Willie, but was the more complete footballer. He not only won the ball, but then used it well. He was like a Scottish version of England's World Cup-winning captain Bobby Moore. Martin's range of passes was incredible, and if he had to find a team-mate from 40 yards, he could drop the perfectly-weighted ball right onto his toes. Martin also proved himself as skipper of Manchester United, and he remains the only man to captain cup-winning sides on both sides of the Border, which is a superb achievement.

Martin was just 21 years old when he led us out at Hampden in 1970, but he was so calm that you would have thought he was heading for a kick-about in a public park. A curious parallel between Martin and Willie is that they were loners in their playing days. It was rare for either to socialise with team-mates after games, which was maybe just as well in Martin's case, because all he ever seemed to do was annoy us with his guitar-playing and intelligent use of words. In response to a request for a 'quick word' from a local reporter, Martin replied 'velocity', and walked away. Other players and managers have reputedly done the same since, but Martin was the first, and journalists were inevitably wary of asking him for interviews.

As for the Spanish guitar-playing, it was one of the reasons why we did not push ourselves when it came to asking Martin if he wanted to join us on nights out. On most occasions he would turn up with his guitar, and insist that everyone gathered around to listen to the latest tune he had learned. At one party Martin's younger brother George, who also played for the Dons, got so fed up with the strumming that he smacked our skipper on the nose and sent him flying over the back of a sofa. Before we had the chance to check if Martin was okay, the consummate musician continued to perform his latest Spanish ditty from behind the settee. Martin has remained a close friend, though the guitar is less evident these days.

George Murray was the father-figure of the 1970 team. He

was a straight-laced individual who was wary of joining us on nights out, and we eventually discovered why when he did agree to consume a few beers. As soon as the alcohol took effect, he was a changed man, and he would launch into impersonations of Elvis Presley: his rendition of *Teddy Bear* left us in stitches. Next day back at the club George would be his usual serious self again, and his colleagues were happy with that because he was always the one we turned to for advice if we had problems, on or off the park. He is a wonderful, kindly man.

One man who could not have been described as quiet was Davie 'The Brush' Robb, the genuine hard nut of the 1970 side. Davie was never the most popular of players with the Aberdeen fans, mainly because of his habit of acting like a world-beater one week, then spending 90 minutes falling over the ball the next. If a war started tomorrow though, Davie would be the first man that I would pick to have by my side. He was a warrior when he pulled on an Aberdeen shirt, and he loved acting as the unofficial minder to the rest of us. The Brush nickname came about because his mane of bushy red hair resembled the tail of Basil Brush, the guffawing TV puppet that was a big favourite with the kids. Davie also looked a bit like Irish actor Richard Harris, which provided him with a fillip when he played in the USA later in his career. Olivia Newton-John, beautiful star of the hit movie *Grease*, took a shine to big Davie, and they supposedly became very close for a spell. Davie is too much of a gentlemen to tell us how close that was, but it makes me smile to think that the man who used to batter guys about for fun in the Scottish League could enjoy the dainty pleasure of escorting one of the world's most desirable women.

Eddie Turnbull did not hesitate to employ Davie's battling qualities to Aberdeen's advantage, though sometimes the big man was not all that keen. We were due to play Celtic on one occasion and Eddie told Davie to 'get wired into Bobby

Murdoch', and not to worry if he injured him and incurred the wrath of the referee. 'But what if I get sent off?' asked Davie. 'Don't worry,' the boss assured him. 'They'll miss him more than we'll miss you.'

Davie incurred Eddie's wrath when he came on as a substitute in another game versus Celtic, wearing white boots. This was years before footwear of various shades became the style, and I don't think anyone else in Scotland was wearing them. Davie was worried about how Eddie, a football traditionalist in many ways, would react to his audacity, so he had hidden them beforehand. Eddie sat open-mouthed when he finally saw Davie making his way towards the pitch . . . then slip on the track and fall on to his backside as he struggled to keep his balance in his shiny white boots. Eddie was furious, and he ordered Davie to bin the footwear at the end of the game. 'You're an ugly enough bastard without drawing attention to yourself,' he roared at Davie, while the rest of us battled to stifle our laughter.

Davie, like Tommy McMillan, was an underrated footballer. On his day he could influence games because he had great skill and a real will to win, and he did well enough to earn five caps for Scotland, including playing against England at Wembley.

We were very fortunate to have Jim Forrest in our line-up for the Hampden cup final. Jim was unfairly cast as scapegoat when Rangers suffered a shock defeat at the hands of Berwick Rangers in the Scottish Cup in 1967. He was a prolific scorer for the Ibrox club, so it was definitely a knee-jerk reaction, but it ended as an advantage for Aberdeen. Jim arrived at Pittodrie via Huddersfield, and was still one of the leading frontmen in the country.

His cousin, the late Alec Willoughby, was also at Pittodrie, and they kept themselves to themselves for much of the time. Jim was a great help to me, though, and passed on the value of holding the ball up and bringing team-mates into the play.

Young Arthur Graham, like Derek McKay, retained his place in the team for the final, because he had hit top form at just the right time. Arthur was 17, but benefited from an old head on young shoulders. Peter Weir, one of the heroes of the Aberdeen side that won the European Cup-Winners' Cup in 1983, is often described as the greatest winger in the club's history. Arthur runs him pretty close, and I have to wonder if Weir would have been able to handle the pressure that Arthur was under at such a young age in 1970. Like Weir, Arthur could use both feet well and take on opponents at pace. He was every full-back's nightmare.

Despite being so young, Arthur was one of the main jokers of the squad, and from his first day we had to be wary about letting him near our personal belongings, because we knew he would use them as props for some prank. A couple of years on, Arthur almost induced a heart attack in Jimmy Bonthrone, Eddie Turnbull's assistant who eventually managed Aberdeen. The Dons had gone on a tour to Bermuda, much to the despair of Arthur who had recently married. He looked down in the dumps on the transatlantic flight, and made no secret of the fact that he would have preferred to be honeymooning with his new bride. I was rooming with Arthur and became concerned when he started to shout and bawl that he was going home, and he demanded that I seek out Jimmy Bonthrone so that he could speak to him. I eventually agreed, and when Jimmy and I walked into the room Arthur screamed at us, ran over to the bay window and dived over the balcony. We were on the second floor, so Jimmy and I were understandably concerned by the scene that would be waiting for us when we raced to peek over the balcony. We were therefore mightily relieved to see Arthur floating on his back in the swimming pool below, laughing over his antics. He had worked out that the depth of the pool would make even such a plunge possible, but the event shook his two team-mates.

The XI chosen for Hampden felt fortunate indeed because Aberdeen could field other talented players from their squad. Martin's brother gained the one spot on the bench, but Alec Willoughby – who became so popular during his spell at Aberdeen that primary schoolchildren still play for a cup bearing his name – was injured and had to sit in the stand alongside Jim Whyte, a fine full-back who was also not allotted the credit due to him, Tommy Wilson and Jim Hamilton. My great pal Ian Taylor was also up there, which must have been hard because he had been planted on the bench when the Dons lost to 2-0 to Celtic in the 1967 final.

7

HUMBLING THE HOOPS

'The lap of honour had been cancelled because
of fears it might upset the Celtic supporters'

Beating Celtic in the Scottish Cup final with the Dons was the
greatest thrill in the world. Many footballers say they can't
remember their biggest triumph because it all passed by in a
flash, but I am fortunate as I can recall every second of that
magical day at Hampden as if it happened yesterday. It was the
highlight of my career, even if it did take place at the end of my
first season as an Aberdeen player. At Gleneagles the night
before, a wealthy American businessman who was also in
residence left me baffled when he asked if we were a basketball
team. Even he stood taller than Joe Harper, so all I could do was
laugh before explaining that we were a soccer side preparing to
play in the Scottish Cup final. The American visitor became all
excited, and he promised that if we won the trophy he would lay
on a lavish party for us.

Eddie Turnbull's breakfast bust-up with Bobby Clark apart,
the build-up on the morning of 11 April was pretty much as
always when we were set to play big games in Glasgow. But
Eddie became visibly tense after we entered the dressing-room

to change and to gather our thoughts. It wasn't like Eddie, who was normally the most confident and animated of people ahead of kick-off. George Murray sorted matters by approaching Eddie and saying: 'Boss, why don't you give us that speech that got us going before the game at Celtic Park?' Eddie obliged by delivering probably the most inspiring speech I ever heard from a football manager. The guys who had played against Celtic in the 2-1 league victory a couple of weeks before confirmed it was pretty much along the same lines, making particular mention of Eddie's desire to avoid having to sit in the dressing-room at the end listening to Jock Stein and his men celebrating. It was stirring stuff, and we almost sprinted out on to the pitch when referee Bobby Davidson gave us the call.

The final was watched by a massive crowd of 108,464, the biggest that I played in front of during my career. It seems incredible when I examine pictures of how packed the terraces were. A veritable sea of faces. The fans were even packed tight on the stairways to the terraces, but on the day I did not notice them. I *was* aware of the noise emanating from the thousands of Dons fans to my left when we entered the fray, but then it was a case of getting down to business, and that meant shutting everything else out.

I cannot explain how I managed that; it was just the way I used to handle the pressure surrounding the really big games. We would have enough to worry about because we were up against a cracking Celtic side: Evan Williams, Davie Hay, Tommy Gemmell, Bobby Murdoch, Billy McNeill, John Brogan, Jimmy Johnstone, Willie Wallace, George Connelly, Bobby Lennox and John Hughes, with Bertie Auld coming on as a substitute for the last-named during the game. Seven of them – Gemmell, McNeill, Murdoch, Johnstone, Wallace, Lennox and Auld – had been involved in the Celtic side immortalised as the

Lisbon Lions when they beat Inter Milan 2-1 in Portugal in the European Cup final three years before. They were on their way to another European Cup final that year, having beaten English champions Leeds United 1-0 at Elland Road in the first leg of their semi-final showdown only 10 days before facing us at Hampden. The Celts had also won the title for the fifth season in a row – they would go on to make it nine back-to-back championships – and the League Cup was already on display in the Parkhead trophy room. Aberdeen, on the other hand, were looking to win the Scottish Cup for only the second time since the club were formed in 1903, the solitary triumph coming 23 years before.

It was not surprising that the nation's bookmakers made Celtic 4-11 favourites, while we were priced at a generous 5-1 to lift the cup. When you add in the fact that Derek McKay, Arthur Graham and I were relative rookies playing at that level – the final constituted Arthur's first Scottish Cup-tie – it was easy to understand why we were not rated to lift the silverware. Eddie Turnbull had faith in his men, though, and he demonstrated on the day that he could match the great Stein when it came to tactics. He asked me to play a little behind our main striker Jim Forrest, and to do my best to break forward. Eddie reckoned Jim's pace would pose a lot of problems for Billy McNeill, and it left Celtic sweeper John Brogan with a dilemma. Did he stay in his normal position or step forward and pick me up? Celtic were such an attack-minded side in those days, Eddie was sure they would not pull a midfield player back to mark me, and he was also certain that Brogan would not alter his way of playing. He was right. I was granted the freedom of Hampden, and was able to float about with plenty of time to pick up the ball and lay off passes. It meant that Celtic's full-backs were often forced to move out of position to stop my runs forward to support Jim. That gave Arthur and Derek the extra space they needed to create havoc on the wings, and we went on to run one of the greatest Celtic teams ragged.

It was none other than Bertie Auld who intensified our determination while we were lined up in the tunnel waiting to move onto the Hampden pitch. Auld did not bother to look at us as he shouted: 'Come on lads, let's get this game over. We've got a proper big game coming up.' He was clearly referring to Celtic's European Cup return with Leeds United the following Wednesday, and all the Aberdeen players heard the taunt. After that there was no way we were going to let them beat us. At the end of the game I went straight over to Bertie and said: 'Look forward to your game. We're away out to get blootered and celebrate winning the Scottish Cup.' My chance to ram Bertie's insult down his throat had come earlier, in the 27th minute, when Derek's cross from the right was handled in the Celtic penalty-area by Bobby Murdoch. That was the time of the actual incident, but another nine minutes elapsed before I struck the penalty-kick. The Celtic players went berserk, though it had been clear that Murdoch had stopped Derek's cross getting over to me in the area. Tommy Gemmell was the biggest culprit. He threw the ball at referee Davidson in anger, and he was fortunate not to be sent off. Tommy could be pretty fearsome at times, so it must have been most intimidating for the official. The rest of the Celtic players surrounded Mr Davidson and it all got a bit crazy, but Celtic players attempting to intimidate was nothing unusual at that time. As their haul of trophies under Jock Stein proved, they were a marvellous team, but they could also be a nasty lot.

As the Celtic players did their best to put me off ahead of taking the penalty-kick, I decided that the best thing to do was to show them I wasn't bothered. They fell silent almost to a man when I grabbed the ball and started to play keepy-up on the penalty-spot. It allowed me to blot out the mayhem that was going on around me, and the nine-minute delay actually seemed fairly short. It may have looked as if I was the calmest man on the park, but my stomach was churning. Who wouldn't be nervous taking a first cup-final spot-kick at Hampden in front of 108,000 fans?

When I finally got the chance to take the penalty, there was no doubt in my mind where it was going. I'm a great believer in making a team's main striker take all the penalties, for if he cannot be confident about scoring with a free shot from 12 yards, he should not be on the pitch. I also believe that penalties should never be missed, though I was guilty of that misdemeanour on a few occasions. I would be really cut up when that happened, even if we won the game, because I had missed an easy chance to add to my tally of goals. I had failed with one penalty attempt for Aberdeen at that time, against Airdrie, when I had changed my routine of placing the ball to the goalkeeper's right. I did not make the same mistake again, even if that meant that any keeper who had done his homework would know which way to move. Many hours of practising penalties with the Danish imports at Morton guaranteed that I was always confident I could place the ball well, and strike it firmly. The keeper would have to make an outstanding effort if he wished to save or parry the ball.

After the nine-minute delay at Hampden, Evan Williams hardly moved as I fired the ball low and hard just inside his right post. It's hard to describe my feelings as the ball hit the net, but I raised my arms skywards and my heart was soaring at the tremendous thrill. Most Scottish boys dream about one day scoring in a cup final at Hampden, and my dream had come true.

Derek McKay added to my exhilaration by whispering as we wandered back to the halfway line: 'Well Joe, if that's the winner you will be able to have any woman you like in Aberdeen tonight!' There was still a long way to go, however, and we were up against a Celtic team now feeling as if they had been hard done by. They piled on the pressure, but Bobby Clark, Martin Buchan and Tommy McMillan played the games of their lives, and at no point did we feel as if our lead was in danger. The only real scare arose when Bobby Lennox blatantly punched the ball out of Bobby Clark's hands, then popped it into the net. The 'goal' was chalked off, despite my fearing for a second or so that the referee would allow it to stand. The referee's appropriate decision sparked more protests from the Celtic players, who did their best throughout the game to intimidate the officials, and the Glasgow side's hopes of a comeback died in the 83rd minute when Derek scored what I still reckon to be the best goal fashioned by an Aberdeen player in a cup final.

Derek was just outside our area when the ball broke into his path, and he flicked it deftly to knock it away from a Celtic player out to the right wing. Derek then raced up to regain possession before playing the ball down the line to me. I spotted Jim Forrest free out on the other wing, and fired a pass over to him. Jim raced forward and hit a shot from a tight angle which Williams could only parry, and Derek, who had made a great run from well inside our half, was on hand to tap the rebound into the net. We were convinced that was it, but Celtic made us jittery by getting a goal back through Bobby Lennox deep in injury-time. Derek was not finished, though.

We broke clear again with Arthur Graham eventually playing the ball to me on the right. I managed to wriggle my way into the Celtic area, and considered shooting until I spotted Derek unmarked to my left. I rolled the ball into his path, Derek controlled it with his left foot then hammered it past Williams with his right, and the Scottish Cup belonged to Aberdeen. I was stunned for a few moments, then close to tears because I was thinking of how proud my parents would be as they looked on

from the Hampden stand. Derek soon brought me down to earth
by saying: 'Hey Joe, remember how that goal of yours was going
to get you any woman you want? Well I've scored two, so you
can forget it!' It was typical of a man who had quickly become
one of my closest pals.

To be fair to the Celtic players, when the whistle was blown
for the final time they sportingly shook our hands. Jock Stein
made a point of giving Eddie a hug and warmly congratulating
him, which enhanced his standing in my eyes. My best memory
from those few moments was the sight of Eddie running across
the pitch excitedly to hug us one by one. The manager was
never the most demonstrative of characters, so it pleased me
to know that we had made the old fella so happy. Scottish
Football Association officials and the Glasgow police then
managed to spoil things a bit from our point of view. When
Martin went up to receive the cup, we noticed that the red-and-
white ribbons were missing, and I was told later that the SFA
people had taken only green-and-white ones because they had
been so sure that Celtic would triumph. We did not wish that
omission to spoil our fun, and I was jumping up and down like
a schoolboy as I watched Martin raise the cup above his head
and point in the direction of the sea of celebrating Dons fans.
We borrowed a red-and-white scarf from a nearby supporter to
use as makeshift ribbon before Martin led us down the Hampden steps to begin our lap of honour, but we were stopped in
our tracks by officials and police. They told us that the lap of
honour had been cancelled because of fears it might upset the
Celtic supporters.

I could be wrong, but I reckon we are the only cup-winning
side who were denied the special experience of parading the
trophy to our fans at Hampden. We protested strongly, and even
attempted to ignore instructions and to start a lap of honour.
The constabulary made it clear, however, that they would have

none of it, and they practically frog-marched us down the tunnel into our dressing-room. Our celebrations were soon in full swing and Arthur Graham threw Jimmy Bonthrone fully clothed into the bath, though the plunge was not the height that had caused such concern in Bermuda. Beer and champagne flowed as the enormity of what we had achieved began to sink in, and my first duty after I had drunk my fill was to seek out my parents and to present them with my winners' medal. It was one of the proudest moments of my life that the achievement had made my mother and father so happy. The fury felt over the absence of a lap of honour dissipated when we finally made our way out of Hampden with the cup. Celtic fans still milling about outside offered a loud ovation in congratulating us, and I'm certain that a similar reaction would have been the outcome inside the stadium, but we did not get the chance to find out.

We returned to the peaceful surroundings of Gleneagles, and our American friend was true to his word with no expense spared as we enjoyed the party of our lives. All was not as it seemed, though, for Derek and I had decided to shower quickly and to get back down to the reception area for a quiet beer before the rest of the lads joined us. We arrived just in time to spot hotel staff removing printed losers' menus, which listed salad and a cold buffet, and instead providing those for winners, which set out dishes for the connoisseur. It was a *great* party, and it was enhanced by a gesture from Arthur Graham, who offered his medal to Dons' scout Bobby Calder, who had convinced the club to give the young man a chance. Bobby declined politely, but we were impressed by Arthur's thoughtfulness.

My head was thumping as we made our way back to Aberdeen by coach the following day. We were told that a street parade had been arranged, which constituted a first for the city, so no one knew quite what to expect. Club officials decided to take us to Stonehaven, south of Aberdeen, beforehand because Billy Meldrum, who owned the Royal Hotel, was a great friend to everyone at Pittodrie. We were pleasantly surprised to see the streets of the coastal burgh packed with people applauding and cheering as we passed, but that was nothing compared to what awaited us in Aberdeen.

When we got to the outskirts of the city, our bus drew into a lay-by just off the dual carriageway in the famous Kincorth district, to allow us to transfer to a single-deck with the roof open so that we could all enjoy a view from on top. It was only later that city officials decided there might be a need to invest in a proper open-top vehicle.

Fears of falling off our victory wagon were soon forgotten as we made our way across the Bridge of Dee and proceeded up Holburn Street. Aberdonians were perched here, there and everywhere, hanging out of windows cheering and shouting and lining the streets. When we reached the top of Holburn Street and turned right into Union Street, the sight that greeted the victorious team left a huge lump in my throat. The one-mile length of Union Street was packed solid, and reports estimated that more than 100,000 souls turned out to greet us. The glorious crush was such that our bus could but crawl towards the top end of the street. Squatting atop that bus produced an unbelievable feeling of euphoria, which remains solid in my heart. We finally made it to the Castlegate, and we were conducted to the balcony of the Town House to display the Scottish Cup and to acknowledge the adulation from our followers packed like sardines below. Someone issued a reminder that it was Eddie Turnbull's birthday, information that was relayed to the crowd, who broke into a spontaneous rendition of 'Happy Birthday'.

The old man looked close to tears. It was a special moment. We rejoined the bus to chug down King Street, which was also lined by cheering supporters, towards Pittodrie. When we finally reached our home, another 20,000 fans were waiting to give us a standing ovation as we walked around the pitch. I lost count of how many times we made the circuit, but it was a day of special significance in a footballer's life, and we did not wish it to end.

We had two league fixtures to fulfil before the season ended, and Hibs gave us a standing ovation when we visited Easter Road on the Monday after the final. We repaid them by winning 2-1 thanks to goals from Davie Robb and Jim Forrest. We also won 2-0 at Motherwell, Jim netting both, so that we headed into the summer of 1970 convinced we were at the start of something big for Aberdeen.

As a footnote to that notable cup final of 1970, and taking account of other fixtures with the Old Firm, I must say that in almost every game that I played against Celtic I experienced players whispering in my ear messages such as: 'I'm going to do you.' Judging by some of the tackles they put in at times, they did their best to render such threats meaningful. Aye, they were a mean lot those Celtic lads, but they were still angels compared to the real hard man of the Scottish game at that time, Rangers' captain John Greig. I must emphasise that John did not go out deliberately to hurt opponents – it was just that when he tackled you it felt as if you had been hit by a double-decker bus. There has never been anyone more committed to the Ibrox cause than John, and I have the scars on my legs to prove it. Despite knowing that I would probably be in pain for days afterwards, I used to look forward to the tussles with him and the rest of the Rangers side, who were only marginally softer than their in-spirational skipper. I recall one game at Ibrox when John taunted me by repeatedly saying: 'This is so easy, I'm smoking a cigar' while gesturing that he was puffing away on a big Havana every time he managed to nip in and take the ball away from me. The roles were reversed when I scored a goal, and I wandered up to John, made the same gesture and said: 'Hey big man, do you have a light?' I knew I would have to be wary of John's lunges for the rest of that game.

On another occasion, when the imposing figure of Tom 'Tiny' Wharton was refereeing, John was particularly robust. I lost count of the number of times that he booted me into the air, then volleyed me on the way down. Rangers were giving us a doing and it was pelting with rain, so I became increasingly frustrated as the minutes ticked away. With little time left, John took possession of the ball in one of the corners with his back to me, and I decided enough was enough. I prescribed John a touch of his own medicine by lunging in at him from behind. It was a terrible tackle, and it sent John flying off the pitch and on to the track. I knew by the contact that I had made that I had hurt him, and his screams of agony confirmed that. As Tiny and I stood over John while he was receiving treatment, the Rangers legend snarled: 'Harper you little bastard. See when I get up, I'm going to break both your fu***** legs off and stuff them up your backside.' I asked Tiny, who was in fact a giant of a man: 'Did you hear what he just said?' I was hoping that the referee would protect me and order John off, but he retorted: 'I believe he was talking to you, Mr Harper.' The man with the whistle wandered away having a quiet laugh to himself, and the remaining minutes of the game were spent avoiding the ball and thus not running the risk of retribution from John Greig, who was now limping.

The speed with which I raced down the tunnel on the final whistle would have rivalled that of an Olympic sprinter. It was all part of the fun, though I avoided laughing the day a Rangers player spat in my face after I had scored a goal. It almost caused a riot, because I went for him and had to be restrained by team-mates. I have not spoken to that Rangers man since because I regard spitting as despicable and cowardly. I have chosen not to name him, because he went on to become well-known as a manager in the Scottish game. He knows who he is.

8

Title Burn-out

*'No matter how hard I worked, the
goals just would not come'*

The squad that won the Scottish Cup for Aberdeen in 1970
should have been crowned Scottish champions the following
year, but I'm afraid we blew it big style. I still look back on the
1970-71 season with anguish, because we had the title within
our grasp and threw it all away as the finishing line beckoned.
My disappointment is all the more intense as I had managed 19
league goals up to the start of February to keep the pressure on
Celtic, but failed to score another in the championship for the
remainder of that season.

Coincidentally the drought had started when Pittodrie Stadium was left badly damaged by a fire in the Main Stand. Three
firemen risked their lives to rescue the Scottish Cup from the
inferno, which lit up the skyline over Aberdeen on the night of
5 February 1971. We were away preparing for our game at
Dunfermline the following day, so it was the Sunday before we
got the chance to survey the damage. A terrible sight met our
eyes. The blaze had all but destroyed the stand, and the dressing-
rooms beneath were gone. Club record books and memorabilia
also went up in smoke, so it was most upsetting for everyone

who worked there, and it caused serious disruption to our way of working. Team spirit was harmed because we tended to report for training with only a few minutes to spare as there was nowhere left for us to socialise. The gymnasium had been converted into a temporary changing-and kit-room, so few of us hung about at the end of training sessions either. And the showers were no more.

Prior to the fire we had been a sociable lot who were happy to spend extra time at the stadium, taking part in games of head tennis and the like, or simply chatting. It would be wrong to blame my dearth of goals over the final three months of the campaign solely on the after-effects of the fire, but I can't help wondering if it affected me, even subconsciously. Eddie Turnbull certainly blamed the conflagration, for it destroyed the machine he used to weigh each of us every day. He has always pointed to my weight, a problem throughout my career, which was allowed to creep up and which he maintained took a bit of the sharpness out of my game. Perhaps there is some truth in that; otherwise I cannot explain why things went so wrong for me.

We had made a stuttering start to the season, which was kicked off by the Scottish League Cup, the teams divided into sections of four. Steve Murray, a talented midfielder who had signed from Dundee in the closing weeks of the previous season, scored in a disappointing draw at Airdrie. We managed to beat St Johnstone home and away, then drew 1-1 with Hibs at Pittodrie, which left them heading our group on goal difference with two games remaining. Goals were obviously needed, so I was pleased to deliver four as we hammered Airdrie 7-3 at Pittodrie to wipe out Hibs' advantage and leave us needing only a draw in the final match in Edinburgh to make the quarter-finals. The game was a nightmare. Pat Stanton put the home side ahead after just seven minutes, and we were hammered 4-0 and hustled out of the competition. Interest in the League Cup was amazing: Easter Road drew a crowd of 24,900 that night, and attendances were also massive for the semis and finals. It's a shame that the tournament has been devalued since by the removal of the carrot of European qualification for the winners and the bigger clubs fielding reserve sides.

Despite our poor initial showing, we were all confident that we were capable of giving Celtic a real fight for the title. That confidence looked misplaced when Airdrie, the team we had dismantled in the League Cup seven days previously, drew 1-1 at Pittodrie in the opening league match of the season. We won 2-1 at Dundee with Joe Harper heading in one of the goals, and making his debut for the Dons was a gangling centre-half named Willie Young, with whom I developed a love-hate relationship.

Willie, who later played for Tottenham Hotspur and won the FA Cup with Arsenal, was a beast of a defender, and I would never question his commitment to the cause. But we did not hit it off on a personal level away from the park, mainly because I felt Willie was a bit of a bully towards those who were not as big as he was, which meant almost everyone. Feeling between us came to a head when a group of players, Willie and me included, went to the Brentwood Hotel planning to watch a live game on television. Two elderly ladies who were resident at the hotel were tuned in to *Coronation Street* on the other channel, and most of the group accepted that. I was brought up to show respect to my elders, and was prepared to move on to watch the game elsewhere. While we were finishing our drinks, Willie began making rude remarks to the ladies in what I saw as an attempt to scare them off and allow us access to the TV. I told him that he was out of order, and the disagreement escalated to the point where he challenged me to a fight outside. Willie is a massive man, close to 6ft 5in tall, but there was no way that I would back down, particularly when I felt I was in the right. When we reached the car park behind the hotel, I threw myself at

Willie and was fortunate to knock him to the ground. I'm not proud to admit that I began rubbing his face hard into the gravel surface of the car park. We were eventually pulled apart and Willie's face was in a bit of a mess, so it's of little surprise that we were not close friends from that day on. We were still team-mates, though, and professional enough not to allow personal differences to affect how we went about our jobs.

Willie stayed in the team for our next game, when we drew 0-0 with St Johnstone at Pittodrie. Those two points dropped at home in the first three games would ultimately prove expensive, but we finally sorted ourselves out and I scored in a 4-0 win at Kilmarnock and in a 3-0 defeat of Hibs at Pittodrie to draw us level with Celtic at the top. The title chase was on. We also had the minor matter of contesting the European Cup-Winners' Cup, and it pains me to recall that we went on to make history for all the wrong reasons in that competition. We were drawn against Hungarian side Honved, which immediately sparked talk of Ferenc Puskas, the magical Magyar who had become an instant hero in Scotland when he helped Hungary to hammer England at Wembley in 1953. I was thrilled that my first crack at continental European opposition – my debut at that level for Morton had been against Chelsea – would come against such a prestigious club, but once again my hopes looked set to be dashed after another accident left me badly cut and stitched up.

I was attending a party at a friend's house on the Saturday night before the Honved game, and two blokes got into a fight. I stepped between them in an effort to break it up, only to be pushed out of the way by the wife of one of the protagonists. I fell backwards into a glass door, and it shattered as I fell through. At first I did not think that I had been hurt for I was feeling no pain, but guests spotted blood pouring down my back. My shirt and the floor had turned bright red, and lifting the shirt tail revealed a nasty big gash in my back. I was rushed to hospital where six stitches were inserted in the wound. Suffering injury in a freak incident was bad enough, but I was obliged to visit Eddie Turnbull's house the following day to tell him that if I was to face Honved, it would be with half-a-dozen stitches in my back. The gaffer, understandably, was upset and I reckoned that he did not totally believe my story; he would be wondering whether I had got drunk and merely fallen through the glass door. I was telling the truth, however, and I was delighted when Eddie decided that I would just have to grit my teeth and get on with it. The wound was painful and in an awkward position on my back, which meant that if I moved my arms or stretched too much the stitches were in danger of popping. It was nothing in comparison to what I had suffered in the car crash during the previous season, though, so I was confident that I would be able to do a job on the pitch.

I received a scare early on when a Honved player whacked me in the back as he went for a high ball. It was very painful, but the stitches held, and that game ended up being one of the most enjoyable in which I featured for Aberdeen, an experience made all the more magical because I scored a goal which is included on my list of career favourites. We delighted most of the 21,500 fans packed into Pittodrie for the first leg with a 3-1 win, and appropriately, I suppose, my goal was a carbon copy of the famous strike by Puskas against the English, when he dragged the ball back, away from Billy Wright, then smacked it into the net. The ball fell to me in the penalty-area, and I pulled it back from a defender to place it past the goalkeeper to make the score 2-1. Steve Murray got our third late on, and we were convinced that would be enough to see us through in the second leg in Hungary. It might well have been, but for the worst display of refereeing that I ever witnessed. Concetto Lo Bello was the Italian official who handled the return match in Budapest, and I believe that we were cheated that night – there is no other way to put it. Honved's first goal, from Kocsis, was at least seven yards offside. That is no exaggeration, and there was no doubt, for the linesman raised his flag to indicate that Kocsis was offside. We were furious when the referee told him to put his flag down and awarded a goal.

Now there was much talk of corruption in European football at that time with tales rife about referees taking bribes. I am certainly not saying that Mr Lo Bello received a bung, for I could never prove that, but what is indisputable is that he gave Aberdeen nothing that night, and we became increasingly angry as the game progressed. Our fury was at boiling point when Honved were awarded a free-kick at the edge of the area with the score at 2-0. Kocsis made a mess of his effort, but the referee quickly ordered him to retake it. This time the ball flew past goalkeeper Bobby Clark, and we were suddenly heading for the exit door. Steve Murray saved us with a goal in the 77th minute to make it 4-4 on aggregate, taking the tie into extra-time. No further scoring meant that Honved and Aberdeen became the first clubs in Europe to decide a competitive match on penalties, which UEFA had decided to introduce at the start of that season. It was certainly a better proposition than the previous method, which had seen ties decided by the toss of a coin, but then we had not spent much time contemplating the prospect of our progress depending purely on penalty-kicks.

Executing a penalty-kick would be no bother to Jim Hermiston or me, who were used to such a duty, but I doubted if some of our team-mates had been required to take even one before Budapest. As I looked around they certainly looked horrified at the prospect. Clubs now practise penalties with shoot-outs in mind, but it was a new concept in 1970, so I'm afraid that we had not bothered to make plans. I was pleased to put my penalty away, and was soon followed by Jim Hermiston. Jim Forrest was not so lucky – he smashed our third attempt against the crossbar – and Honved proved the better team in the shoot-out by 5-4. It was their goalkeeper Bertalan Bicskei who cracked the decisive kick past Bobby Clark. Penalty shoot-outs are now commonplace, and I have to say that I love watching them . . . though I was a member of the first team to suffer defeat in that way.

Back then my mood became even darker when we visited my old club Morton the following Saturday in the league. Aberdeen lost 2-0 and I was sent off, which brought a lot of stick from the Morton fans, many of whom were my pals. My feeble excuse was that I was being kicked all over the place by the Cappielow defenders. Suffice it to say that when the hosts netted their second goal I lost the plot and had a go at the referee, with the result that I was away for an early bath. I made amends a couple of weeks later by scoring when we beat Rangers 2-0 at Ibrox – a sweet experience for any Aberdeen player. We won 3-1 at St Mirren the following weekend, which was significant because that would be the last time we would lose a goal in the league until the middle of January, and we had reached only the end of October. As stated earlier, the amazing run lasted for 12 games, 19 hours and 15 minutes in all, which constituted a British record for league shut-outs. Bobby Clark, Henning Boel, Jim Hermiston, Martin Buchan and Tommy McMillan were never better, and they inspired the rest of us to raise our games. We scored 31 goals in those 12 matches, which amounted to an astonishing run that had everyone at Pittodrie buzzing with excitement.

Six successive fixtures were won with ease, and I claimed a hat-trick in a 7-0 demolition of Cowdenbeath at Pittodrie. That ensured we travelled to Celtic at the start of December 1970 with the chance of overtaking them at the top of the table. Newspapers were predicting that Aberdeen would be put in their place, but Eddie Turnbull was quick to point out that we had won the away league game the previous season just ahead of our victory over Jock Stein's men in the Scottish Cup final. He told us that if we really had ambitions to be champions, then this encounter was vital. We responded just as Eddie wished, winning 1-0 thanks to one of my best goals for the Dons. Early in the second half Jim Hermiston sent a long throw into their area, and Davie Robb rose above a posse of Celtic defenders at the front post to nod the ball on. When it reached me in front of goal an acrobatic diving header sent the ball into the net like a bullet. Celtic threw everything at us, but our defence was fire-proof and we held out to take the two points and leapfrogged Stein's side to the top of the league. Indeed, the amazing run of form saw us notch up 15 straight wins in all competitions, and we were convinced that it would be our season to be crowned the best in the land.

While riffling through my collection of press cuttings to piece together information for this book, I was amused to note that I was interviewed in November 1970 for a 'Meet the Player' feature in the *Green Final,* the sports paper that was formerly published by the *Evening Express* in Aberdeen. I think that it makes for amusing reading in retrospect, so it is quoted in full:

> There were some football fans who thought that £40,000 was too big a sum to pay for a player from Morton who hadn't hit it off in English football. But even this minority must now be fully convinced that Joe Harper, Aberdeen's wee buzz bomb, was worth every penny. Joe has been in great form this season and looks as if he will take a bit of beating in the race for top scorer in the First Division.

AGE: 22. Height, 5ft 6in. Weight, 11st 5lbs.

WHEN SIGNED: 1969.

PREVIOUS CLUB: Morton (twice), Huddersfield.

FAVOURITE PLAYER: Pele.

FAVOURITE TEAM (apart from Aberdeen): Rangers.

FAVOURITE GROUNDS: Pittodrie and Cappielow.

BEST PLAYER FACED: Bobby Moore.

MOST MEMORABLE OCCASION: 1970 Scottish Cup final.

TIP FOR THE TOP: Joe Smith, Aberdeen.

LIKES: Good music.

DISLIKES: Football critics who have never played the game.

HOBBIES: Golf, table tennis.

FAVOURITE SINGERS: Male – Frank Sinatra, Dean Martin. Female – Lulu, Mama Cass.

FAVOURITE FILM STARS: Male – Steve McQueen, Paul Newman. Female – Ann-Margret.

FAVOURITE GROUP: Four Tops.

FAVOURITE TV PROGRAMMES: Joe likes all sports programmes.

AMBITIONS: To do all he can to help Aberdeen win the Scottish League this season.

MAN HE ADMIRES MOST: Professor Christian Barnard, the South African heart transplant surgeon.'

Current *Evening Express* sports editor Charlie Allan, who helped me to write this book, has ridiculed me for the admission that Rangers were my other favourite team. If that were true, it could leave me in danger of being lynched by the Dons fans who came to adore me over the years, because as far as the Aberdeen faithful are concerned, Rangers form the arch-enemy.

It isn't true, though. I will always be a big fan of Morton, and I have argued with Charlie that the 1970 article, which I assume was written by the legendary Jimmy Forbes, who covered all Aberdeen's games at the time, got it wrong. Perhaps Jimmy, who had a very strong relationship with Eddie Turnbull, put in Rangers as a wind-up. It pleases me, however, to see that I chose Joe Smith as the one to watch. He was a young lad trying to move out of the shadow of his older brother Jinky, a marvellous talent who transferred to Newcastle United in 1970 after making his name with the Dons. Joe eventually proved that the Smith family had more than one footballing talent in the ranks by helping Aberdeen to win the League Cup in 1976, which showed that I must have known what I was talking about all those years ago!

My ambition to help the Dons to win the title in 1970-71 looked to be on course because by the turn of the year we were four points clear of Celtic, who had a game in hand. Our defence had conceded only seven goals in 21 games and we were brimming with confidence. Pat Stanton – a future team-mate at Hibs who would also become my assistant manager at Aberdeen – finally breached our defence in the 64th minute of our clash at Easter Road, and we went on to lose 2-1. We seemed to have recovered when we beat Morton 3-1 at Pittodrie in our next game; I got two goals to rub in the misery felt by some of my old Cappielow mates. Six days later, however, Pittodrie went up in smoke, and that was the start of a downward spiral for the team and for me.

I trained normally and put in the same effort, but no matter how hard I worked, the goals just would not come. It forms a period that haunts me to this day. Bobby, Martin, Tommy and the other guys at the back had done their bit by performing heroically during the first part of the campaign to help us reach pole position in the title race. It was my turn to make a contribution to push us over the finishing line, but I failed. Bobby and I were fortunate to pick up league-winners' medals in

1979-80, our last season as Aberdeen players, but the rest of the squad from 1970-71 were not so lucky. And it's particularly tragic that Martin Buchan and Tommy McMillan did not receive accolades for proving that they were among the best central defensive partnerships that the Scottish game had seen during that record-breaking run of shut-outs. We drew the next two home games, 0-0 with Rangers and 1-1 with St Mirren, and Celtic faltered as well by drawing at Hearts. But we could sense that good fortune was starting to slip away from us.

Rangers ended our reign as Scottish Cup-holders when their defender Colin Jackson – who had attended school in Aberdeen – scored the only goal in our quarter-final tie at Ibrox. That left the league as our only hope of glory, but I was not doing a lot to help to achieve that, though Jim Forrest and Davie Robb were compensating by delivering their fair share of goals.

Jim got his 200th strike at the top level in Scotland when we won 4-1 against Ayr at Pittodrie, which was a remarkable achievement. Big Davie followed that with an outstanding hat-trick when we came back from a goal down to beat Hearts at Tynecastle. That meant we were guaranteed to take the title if we won our remaining four games, which included a home clash with Celtic.

The first of those was a Pittodrie encounter with Motherwell, and we were angry with ourselves for failing to make home advantage count. It turned out to be an awful game, and I had a stinker yet again. George Buchan hit the Motherwell crossbar with a late header, but it ended 0-0 and meant that we now had to overcome Celtic, or it would be all over. Lady Luck offered us a helping hand the following weekend when we won 2-1 at Cowdenbeath, despite another woeful performance. They were bottom of the table and already relegated, but it took an own-goal and a late header from George Buchan, which went in this time, to steal the points.

Our disappointment at having played so poorly at Central Park soon disappeared when we learned that Celtic had managed to gain only a 1-1 draw at home to Dundee United. A victory over the Celts at Pittodrie the following weekend would see Aberdeen crowned Scottish champions for the first time since 1955. It was a league decider that has been almost forgotten with the passing of the years. Aberdeen are criticised for blowing their title chances on the last day of the 1990-91 season at Ibrox, yet we were better off 20 years before that because the decisive game was on our own patch, and we had lost just three of our previous 32 league fixtures in that season.

Pittodrie was sold out within hours and 35,000 fans squeezed in to witness what would have been the greatest Dons win at their own stadium. I was aggrieved to find myself on the bench for such a massive encounter, but poor form and a series of niggling injuries meant that I was hardly in a position to complain. Harry Hood silenced the massed Aberdeen support by hooking home the opening goal for Celtic after just three minutes. Alec Willoughby equalised before the interval, but no matter how hard we tried, we could not nail the second goal that would have made us champions. The closest we got was when an Arthur Graham shot struck Billy McNeill on the Celtic goal-line and bounced clear. I eventually got on the park in place of George Buchan, but my shooting boots were still posted missing, and it was positively gut-wrenching to watch the Celtic players celebrate because drawing 1-1 at Pittodrie meant the destination of the championship trophy was back in their hands. We were still three points ahead, but Celtic had two games in hand, and my failure to find the net since January also meant that the Celts held a significant lead over us if the title was to be decided on goal difference, which was still a possibility.

Falkirk, with Alex Ferguson playing up front, shattered our hopes by beating us 1-0 at Brockville in our final game. Even more frustrating was the fact that Celtic drew 2-2 at St Mirren the following midweek, which meant that they would have been under intense pressure if we had beaten the Bairns. We had let them off the hook, and a 2-0 win over Ayr United followed by a 6-1 hammering of Clyde at Celtic Park tied up their title by two points.

I was devastated. I felt that we might well have taken the championship if I had been able to keep the goals flowing. We were highly praised in the media for running the greatest Celtic side of all time so close. We were undefeated in the 17 league games played at Pittodrie that season and conceded only seven goals in front of our own fans; losing only four times on our travels also demonstrated that we were a side to be reckoned with. Nevertheless, the silverware had remained beyond our grasp. Despite my despair, I was soon thinking ahead and dreaming of making up for what had happened by helping the Dons to win the title the following season. But the wind was knocked out of my sails before the 1971-72 campaign had kicked off when Eddie Turnbull revealed that he had decided to quit Aberdeen and to return to the club of his first love, Hibernian.

9

A Boot Cast in Bronze

❖

*'My tally of 33 league goals was a
post-war record for the Dons'*

I was absolutely gutted when Eddie Turnbull called us into a
team meeting to announce that he was leaving to become
manager of Hibs. Some of us were close to tears when the gaffer
gathered us around after his final training session to explain why
he had decided to move on, but we understood his reasons. He
was one of the greats at Easter Road as a player, continued to
have great affection for the Edinburgh club, and probably would
have regretted it for the rest of his life if he had turned down their
offer. All that was no consolation to those he would leave
behind, because we knew things would never be quite the same
without the man who had transformed Pittodrie during seven
years in charge.

The Dons appointed as the new boss Jimmy Bonthrone, who
had been Eddie's trusted assistant, but that was a big mistake. I
don't wish to be disrespectful to Jimmy, who died in June 2008
while I was writing this book, for he was a gentleman and one of
the most pleasant people I met in football, but that was also his
biggest problem. Jimmy was the perfect No. 2, the figure that
players felt comfortable about approaching if they had problems

with any of Eddie's decisions. I hate to say it, but I just did not feel that he was sufficiently ruthless to succeed as No. 1. Jimmy was always great to me, but he did not appear comfortable after promotion.

Jimmy made the perfect start, though, by leading Aberdeen to victory in the Drybrough Cup, a competition that had been launched that season 24 hours after he had taken over from Eddie. It was run along the lines of the Watney Cup, which had been successful in England, entrants being the eight teams who had scored the most goals in the previous campaign. It was a straight knock-out format and provided an ideal opportunity to prepare for the new season, far better than a mundane series of friendly games.

We travelled to East Fife on the last day of July 1971 and won 3-0 thanks to goals from me, George Buchan and Arthur Graham. That booked a trip to Airdrie where we again won comfortably by 4-1, George, Alec Willoughby, Davie Robb and an own-goal completing our tally. Celtic made it through in the other half of the draw to set up a mouth-watering final at Pittodrie, which attracted a capacity crowd of 28,000. Jock Stein later tried to belittle our 2-1 victory over his team by claiming that he was not too worried because he 'wasn't enamoured in any way by the Drybrough Cup'. The Celtic players certainly showed commit-ment to the competition during the final as they attempted to kick lumps out of us in one of the roughest Aberdeen v Celtic battles in which I played. Davie Robb put us ahead in the 20th minute, an effort negated by a John Hughes strike, and I had the honour of scoring the winner after Tom Callaghan had chopped me down just inside the Celtic penalty-area. I slotted the spot-kick into the net to the right of goalkeeper Evan Williams, just as I had done when we won the Scottish Cup final.

Bedlam ensued on the final whistle as home fans spilled onto the Pittodrie pitch, among them my co-author Charlie Allan, who was an excited 13-year-old supporter on the day. Charlie claims that he asked me if he could have my shirt as a souvenir, but things were so crazy that I cannot recall the request. After relative calm had been restored, Martin Buchan received the cup at the front of the Main Stand, and that set us up for the start of our League Cup campaign. Or so we believed.

We were drawn in a section with Falkirk, Dundee and Clyde, who had all finished well behind us in the league the previous season. Aberdeen were expected to top the group and to make it to the quarter-finals with ease, but the opening game against Dundee at Pittodrie produced a 1-1 draw. I scored in victories over Clyde home and away and over Falkirk at Pittodrie, but a 3-1 defeat inflicted by Dundee at Dens Park left us needing at least a draw in our last match – away to the Bairns – to claim a quarter-final clash against Hibs, now Eddie Turnbull's side. Alex Ferguson played one of his finest matches for Falkirk and scored twice as they won 3-1 to advance to the last eight. We finished in third spot, in the wake of Dundee, which did not go down well with our supporters.

I was determined to contribute more once the league campaign got under way, and I made a personal vow that I would not allow the goals to dry up in the midst of a season again. I must confess that progress was far better than even I had expected, and I finished the campaign with 33 goals, a total which was sufficient to earn me the coveted Bronze Boot, which is awarded to leading scorers in the European game. I was beaten to the gold award by Gerd Müller of Bayern Munich and West Germany, who scored 40 times in the Bundesliga. Antonis Antoniadis of Panathinaikos in Greece came second with 39 goals. I was only the second British player to reach the top three – the other being Celtic's Bobby Lennox in 1968 – so I was mighty proud of the achievement. My Bronze Boot now resides in a cabinet in the Pittodrie boardroom, and I enjoy glancing at it from time to time, though I had to pass up the award ceremony in France at the start of the following season because Aberdeen were involved in a midweek League Cup-tie.

The first of the 33 goals was a gem, though I say so myself, and it came as our last strike in a 3-0 win over Dundee at Pittodrie when I dribbled past two defenders on the left and cut inside to belt an unstoppable shot past the goalkeeper. My fears about Jimmy being the right man to take over from Eddie Turnbull appeared to be unfounded as we went on to win eight and draw two of our opening ten league games to rise to the top of the table, a point ahead of Celtic.

We also recorded a notable victory over Spanish side Celta Vigo in the UEFA Cup. The Spanish league was regarded as far stronger than the Scottish version, so we were not expected to make much of an impression against Celta, who had remained undefeated at home over the previous season. We were drawn away in the first leg, and our hopes of victory dipped when we learned that travel problems would result in the French referee being assisted by two Spanish linesmen. A well-drilled off-side trap was one of our main ploys in vital away games, so we were understandably concerned that the local officials might not give us the benefit of the doubt with marginal decisions. We decided to sit in a bit deeper than normal instead and to hit the Spaniards on the break, and it worked a treat. I put us ahead early in the second half with a well-placed lob from the edge of the penalty-area, then Jim Forrest scored direct from a corner-kick and we won 2-0 to clinch Aberdeen's most significant victory in Europe up to then.

We were delighted, but our post-victory enjoyment was spoiled somewhat by the outrageous conduct of a Scottish journalist, who is now dead and will remain anonymous, God rest his soul. He got drunk at our hotel and began to make some disgraceful comments about Arthur Graham. He referred to Arthur coming from Castlemilk, one of the rougher parts of

Glasgow, and he was well out of order. I told him more than once to shut his mouth and to go to his room to sober up, but he went on and on with his diatribe describing Arthur as a 'minker' (a distinctive Scottish word describing a ragamuffin or vagrant) and clearly trying to goad our young team-mate into a response. Arthur could look after himself, but he was still a teenager and no doubt remained a bit wary about what might happen if he had a go at the ill-mannered scribe . . . so I eventually stepped in and laid out the blabbermouth with a right hook. The punch proved effective, though I certainly was not proud of what I had done, but the journalist had overstepped the mark by a considerable distance and deserved the indignity of being carried off in a dazed state by colleagues. Given that many witnesses, including others in the press corps, had been about, I braced myself for stories about the bust-up being emblazoned in the newspapers. It pleases me to record now that this is the first written account to appear describing what happened that night. To their eternal credit, other journalists told me that they agreed their professional pal had been out of order and they had resolved to make no mention of what had taken place. The man who had been laid out apologised to Arthur and me the following morning. I don't think that he received much co-operation from those at Aberdeen FC from that point on.

Victory in Spain gave us confidence for the return game at Pittodrie, but we made heavy work of it. It was my 100th game for Aberdeen, which made missing a penalty all the harder to bear, and we survived a few nervous moments before I ultimately got it right in the last minute and claimed the only goal with a spectacular 25-yard shot. That set up an even bigger tie in the next round against the Italian giants Juventus, who had been beaten finalists the previous season and had just turned striker Pietro Anastasi into the world's first £1m footballer. They were also destined to be crowned Italian champions that season, and the majority of the Italian national side sported the black and white of Juventus in their day jobs, so we knew we would be up against it. The first game was scheduled for Turin, and it may constitute the best 90 minutes of football that I have had the pleasure of watching from afar. I was actually on the pitch, but we were chasing shadows from start to finish as the Italians gave us a lesson in how European football should be fashioned. Anastasi confirmed why Juve had paid a massive sum for his services by racing through from the halfway line to fire a rocket past Bobby Clark after five minutes. Fabio Cappello, who years later would be appointed manager of England, made it 2-0 after 55 minutes with a free-kick that took a deflection on its way past poor Bobby, who was more overworked that night than at any point in his Aberdeen career. We did our best to compete. Willie Young tried a bit too hard, and was replaced by Ian Taylor before the referee could send him off for a spate of fouls, and I too let frustration get the better of me after we had forced our only corner-kick near the end.

Italian international defender Francesco Morini had given me a torrid time from the outset, and though his side were strolling to success that failed to deter him from using dirty tricks to put me off on the few occasions on which the ball appeared in the Juventus half. Scottish footballers tended to be criticised for not possessing the techniques of the Italians or the Germans at that time, but one of Morini's subtle habits was to nip the skin on my back between his fingers as I was about to control the ball. The natural reaction was to flinch a little, and it was enough to make me look daft as the ball struck me in the face or some other part of my anatomy before it returned to the custody of the Italians. I decided it was time for Morini to flinch a little as the corner-kick was being lined up. He was standing just behind me, so I slipped my hand down his shorts, grabbed his private parts and squeezed with all of my might while whispering: 'Take that, you Italian bastard.' Moroni didn't even blink, and I began to wonder if he was some sort of robot. He merely smiled at me, cleared the cross from the corner and departed without a word. I anticipated retaliation from him in the closing minutes, but the battle of subtle techniques was over.

We knew in our hearts that we were unlikely to overcome the 2-0 deficit in the second leg, but the Dons were determined to present a spectacular show at Pittodrie. The Granite City was buzzing for the visit of the Italians, and despite it being the depths of November hardy fans queued overnight to purchase tickets, which were snapped up in record time. The Italians had to endure freezing conditions on a pitch that was sprinkled with snow, but they again proved to be a class above us. The astonishing Anastasi skipped past Martin Buchan to make it 1-0 and 3-0 on aggregate early in the second half, though I at least made sure that we did not succumb at home by heading in an equaliser on 70 minutes. Morini, much to my relief, was pretty subdued in the second encounter, but he pinched the last laugh. As we were making our way off the pitch he indicated that he would be happy to exchange shirts. At the entrance to the tunnel I had my shirt half over my head when Morini grabbed my private parts, squeezed hard and rasped: 'Take that, Mr Harper.' I didn't know whether to laugh or cry.

The Dons were still very much in the race for the league title. One of our more memorable performances at Pittodrie in the lead-up to the end of 1971 was a 7-2 thrashing of Partick Thistle, who had shocked Celtic by 4-1 in the League Cup final the week before. I put together a hat-trick as we prepared perfectly for another crucial visit to Celtic Park. Celtic dominated the game and deserved to be ahead through Harry Hood, but Billy

McNeill deflected a cross into his own net, and we were fortunate to trek home with a 1-1 draw on our record. Celtic's latest teenage sensation Kenny Dalglish was denied late on by a super save from Bobby Clark, and the draw was enough to keep us a point ahead of the Glasgow side at the head of the division.

And yet our form began to stutter as we moved towards the turn of the year. Hearts, despite having a man sent off, became the first team to beat us in the league at Pittodrie for two years when a Donald Ford hat-trick ensured a 3-2 win, but a bigger blow was landed in February when Manchester United swooped to sign Martin Buchan for £125,000. Martin had been an outstanding captain for Aberdeen, so he was bound to move on at some time, but we could not understand our directors' decision to sell him at a crucial stage of the season; despite some faltering, we remained in the hunt for the title and for the Scottish Cup, with a quarter-final beckoning versus Hibs. I am sure that the board should have held on to Martin until the summer, when plenty of offers for such a talented player would still have been on the table.

As if to confirm my contention, Partick Thistle, a team that we had hammered earlier in the campaign, beat us 2-0 at Firhill in our first league game after Martin's departure, and Hibs knocked us out of the cup by a 2-0 margin at Easter Road. I obviously accept that it takes more than one player to make a team tick, but Martin was such a major influence that it was inevitable we would suffer. We were in second spot but five points adrift of Celtic when they visited Aberdeen in March. Bobby Lennox gave the visitors the lead, and I struck in a late equaliser to ensure that we had completed eight games without defeat in recent encounters with Celtic. Our title chance had gone, though.

I took some consolation from the fact that I had done my best to keep the goals coming and added another four as we trounced

Ayr United 7-0 at Pittodrie. My tally of 33 league goals was a post-war record for the Dons, and I was pleased to end the campaign with 42 marked up in all competitions, though I would readily have swapped some for a league-winners' medal. After putting Ayr to the sword, we were frustrated by a 0-0 result at Clyde the following week, and Celtic won 3-0 at East Fife that afternoon to clinch the title for a seventh successive season.

We finished the league programme 10 points behind Celtic, though as runners-up we would be involved in European competition again the following season. Never mind Europe, with Martin Buchan gone I feared that we would find it difficult to sustain a Scottish championship challenge of the type that we had mounted in the previous two seasons. In looking to the future I was unaware that my first spell as an Aberdeen player was approaching a conclusion – after we had completed a crazy end-of-season tour of North America.

10

FIGHTING ON FOREIGN FIELDS

'Berti Vogts was a marvellous player'

Aberdeen's decision to tour North America in the summer of 1972 did not go down well with the majority of players. We had completed our league campaign with a disappointing 0-0 draw against Falkirk on April 29, and we were looking forward to recharging our batteries during the close season.

I was due to marry in July, so the announcement that we would be flying out at the start of May and would not return until the end of June did not please my fiancée Fiona. I suppose the bonus for me was that I missed all the organising that is necessary ahead of a wedding, and I stepped off the plane into the church. I had been made aware that Fiona was upset, so when I reached the other side of the Atlantic I bought two giant stuffed replicas of the main characters from the Disney cartoon musical *Lady and the Tramp*, which I knew she loved. The toys were on sale at the airport when we arrived at Bermuda, and I was worried that I might not see their like on the rest of the tour. I was bit of a novice when it came to world travel, remember, so I drew scorn and laughter when the lads observed that the toys were widely available wherever we visited. I persisted and lugged the precious items around with my luggage from one venue to the next, and the gifts survived despite being captured by heart-less colleagues and kicked around airports and hotels. It tran-spired back in Scotland that Fiona was not impressed because Tramp had an eye and an ear missing and both items were bashed about a bit. Football mates can be so cruel!

The tour was hectic. We completed 12 games between 14 May and 10 June, did not spend more than two days in one spot and lived out of suitcases for the duration. The club gave us $12 a day to spend on lunch and other requisites and we had little time to ourselves. Most of the opposition was on the weak side, so the organisers included four games against Wolverhampton Wan-derers from England in the mid-section of the itinerary, These were played back to back over the space of a week in San Francisco, Seattle, Vancouver and Los Angeles, which meant that we were constantly in the air. Wolves had their strongest side available, including the late, great Derek Dougan, and we won the opening encounters 3-1 and 3-0, then lost 3-0 and 4-0, and the sequence formed the most enjoyable sector of the trip.

The craziest experience came when we travelled to take on Canadian team Montreal Olympics. The venue was packed with fans squeezed behind high fences and the pitch was ringed by police kitted out in riot gear, which is not what you would expect for a friendly game. Montreal included a familiar figure who was spending the summer with them in Scot Graeme Souness, but otherwise comprised mainly Italian players. Most of the specta-tors were also of Italian descent, and we entered an atmosphere which was ugly and intimidating. Early in the second half I was chopped down inside the Montreal penalty-area and scored with the resultant spot-kick to make it 1-0, sparking a riot. Fans attempted to clamber over the fences and pelted us with bottles, cans and anything they could lay their hands on. Davie Robb was knocked over by a large dustbin that had apparently been hurled over the fence; Arthur Graham was pelted by shoes and caused great amusement by stopping play to try one on for size. Which only made matters worse. Armed police were soon rushing in and attempting to restore calm, so we were relieved when the referee told us that he had decided to abandon the game for safety reasons. Armed officers stood on guard outside our dressing-room while spectators were ushered away. We were eventually allowed to leave and Souness kindly invited us to a party with some of his team-mates.

The drama was not over for Arthur Graham and yours truly. While walking back towards our hotel we heard voices coming from what we thought was a bar in a basement. We fancied having a nightcap so went to go down the stairs – only to be met by two powerfully-built black men holding knives which seemed the size of swords. They wanted us to hand over our money, but had not bargained on the speed of reaction of Scottish professional footballers. I reckon it was the only time I outran Arthur in a race as we beat a hasty exit.

The tour ended with a 5-0 win over Boston Astros, the friendly played on a pitch that was marked out for baseball, and we had to take care not to trip over the bases. Astros were owned by a businessman with Italian roots, who treated us to a feast at a seafood bar he owned. We were plonked down at rows of benches and given wooden plates and mallets and fed an array of giant crabs and lobsters, fare that was certainly different from the mince and tatties we were more used to back home. We retired to our host's luxurious offices to savour the delights of his extensive bar, which was bigger than many pubs I know. I mentioned how Arthur and I had been threatened by would-be robbers and asked if there was much trouble of that sort in Boston. 'Never, Joe,' he replied. 'We have our own special way of dealing with trouble.' Our host pressed a button underneath the rim of his desk and the bar behind him opened up . . . to reveal an array of guns, rifles and knives in a case concealed in a secret compartment in the wall. Enough ammunition was available to win a small war. Given that *The Godfather* was the movie of the moment, the obvious question to ask was whether our host was some sort of Mafia boss. Even big Davie Robb wasn't brave enough to do that!

We returned home exhausted, but we were agreed that the trip had lifted our spirits after the disappointment of finishing second on the league yet again. Our summer break was to be the shortest ever at three weeks, and I had to fit a wedding and honeymoon into that. The wedding went off well at Elderslie, Renfrewshire, despite Derek McKay's controversial speech as best man, and the occasion drew a fair bit of press coverage because Fiona was a leading model at the time and was the reigning Miss Grampian TV. We spent a couple of weeks in Spain before I returned to work in time for Aberdeen to start their defence of the Drybrough Cup. I scored the only goal as we overcame St Mirren 1-0 at Pittodrie on July 29, but Celtic gained revenge by beating us 3-2 after extra-time in the semi-final in Glasgow. I was excited by what the season might hold in store because I had a new strike partner in Drew Jarvie, who had been signed from Airdrie.

I maintain that Drew was my best strike partner. He was a vastly underrated footballer who gave the Dons great service, including spells on the coaching staff, and he had a reputation for what he described as shoulder charges on opposing goal-keepers, but which I reckoned were more akin to assaults. It always provided a laugh when Drew protested because a referee had awarded a foul for his latest lunge, usually with the poor goalie rolling about in agony in the goalmouth.

Drew and I hit it off immediately, and he deserves great credit for the fact that I managed to score an astonishing 15 goals in the League Cup alone that season. He also netted 10 League Cup goals, which was an amazing return when you consider that we had played together in only a couple of Drybrough Cup games and two friendlies before the season got under way officially. Drew marked up his first when we started the League Cup section matches with a 4-0 thrashing of Queen of the South in Dumfries, and he and I landed two each as we saw off Hibs 4-1 at Pittodrie. Now many fans have told me that my second that day is their favourite Joe Harper goal for Aberdeen, and I must agree that it was quite spectacular. Hibernian goalkeeper Jim Herriot attempted to play a long ball towards the halfway line, but I was fortunate enough to intercept it. Herriot did his best to back-track towards his goal, but he had no chance because I hit the ball perfectly to send a 40-yard lob over him and into the net. I scored another two when we beat Queen's Park 5-1 at Pittodrie to bring our tally to 13 in just three matches. Hibs ensured we didn't get too carried away by beating us 2-1 at Easter Road and I missed a penalty as we struggled to beat Queen of the South 2-1 at Pittodrie with Ian Purdie grabbing the winner late on, but I made amends for that with a hat-trick as we beat Queen's Park 3-0 at a virtually deserted Hampden to book our spot in the knock-out stages of the competition. We were definitely thinking that we would return to Hampden when the stadium would be a lot busier. I also got the only goal as we beat Hibs at Pittodrie in our opening league fixture, and I was starting to believe that we might be able to cope without Martin Buchan after all.

Aberdeen were boosted by the arrival of Hungarian midfielder Zoltan Varga from Hertha Berlin. He was a gifted player and it was a privilege to play alongside him briefly, but it baffles me that he has since been described as an Aberdeen legend. Zoltan's image even made it onto the painting that the Dons commissioned in 2003 to celebrate the club's centenary. I'm proud that I was included in the work alongside the likes of Willie Miller, Alex McLeish, Gordon Strachan, Graham Leggat, Charlie Cooke and 1930s strikers Willie Mills and Matt Armstrong. I do not believe that Zoltan should have been in the august line-up, especially when you consider that John Hewitt, who scored the winner in the 1983 European Cup-Winners' Cup final, and a good few other important figures were excluded. Zoltan played 31 games for the Dons over a short period and fans still recall the appearance in which he scored twice against Celtic, though we ultimately lost the battle 3-2. I agree that both strikes were spectacular – the first was a swerving 20-yard shot, the second a delightful lob – but the mists of time appear to have clouded the opinions of some.

Zoltan had arrived at Aberdeen amid whispers of being involved in some sort of bribes scandal in Germany, but whenever any of us attempted to ask him about that, he always claimed that his English was too poor to understand the detail of our questions. He was a mysterious man, that's for sure.

Whatever had transpired in Zoltan's previous business, his skills were not sufficient to help us to maintain a challenge to Celtic at the top of the league table. We could manage only a 2-2 draw at home to Falkirk in his debut game after being held by Dundee and St Johnstone and going down 2-1 at Hearts. Dons followers had to be content with the excitement of our League Cup exploits and the fact that we had been handed another bumper draw in the UEFA Cup. We were paired with Borussia Moenchengladbach whose star-studded line-up included future Scotland boss Berti Vogts, Rainer Bonhof, who would serve as his No. 2 in Scotland, and world-class midfielder Gunter Netzer. The latter was the star of the show as the West Germans ran us ragged in the first half of the first leg at Pittodrie, though we were not helped by injury to Bobby Clark, which thrust young Andy Geoghegan – who eventually quit football and worked as a policeman in Aberdeen – into goal. Netzer's skills helped to ensure that Borussia were two up at the interval and we were thankful that he had to leave the field because of a thigh injury. We raised our game after the restart and pulled them back to

2-2, thanks to goals from Drew Jarvie and me. Danish international Henning Jensen put the visitors into a 3-2 lead in the 76th minute and that's how it finished, but we were pleased to have given a decent account of ourselves against opposition of high quality.

Borussia were still favourites to advance to the next round, but we almost pulled off a massive shock in the return leg. The tie was moved to Nuremberg on the orders of UEFA because of a bottle-throwing incident at Borussia's ground the previous season. It proved to be an epic battle and one of the most exciting games in which I featured. We fell further behind with three minutes gone, but struck back with goals from Drew, Alec Willoughby and Steve Murray to reach the interval 3-2 ahead and, much to our astonishment, 5-5 on aggregate.

Unfortunately it was my slip up that handed Borussia the advantage that they sought so desperately. Berti Vogts may well be remembered as the worst Scotland manager, but he was a marvellous player and at the peak of his powers in 1972. Nuremberg provided one of the few interludes in my career when I was asked to forget about scoring goals and to concentrate on matching the opposing full-back's runs forward. Vogts was so effective that if he was allowed too much freedom he would bomb forward and set up chances or score spectacular goals, which he did regularly. I did as I was asked until the 70th minute, when I was caught out of position for the only moment in the game. The ball was played over my head, and that gave Vogts the freedom to stride up the park past Willie Young and to strike a fantastic shot beyond Bobby Clark. I was devastated because my error had allowed the West Germans to take command of the tie again. We needed another goal and were forced to push forward, which allowed Borussia to hit the net twice more inside the final seven minutes to make it 6-3 on the night. The final aggregate score of 9-5 makes crazy reading, but it flattered our opponents. Had it not been for my mistake at a vital moment, I'm convinced that we could have shocked them and made Europe sit up and take notice.

Another highlight from season 1972-73 came with a friendly against Manchester United at Pittodrie in October, which had been agreed as a part of Martin Buchan's transfer deal to Old Trafford. George Best and Bobby Charlton were included in the visiting squad, and it proved to be a memorable night for the capacity crowd. Scotland striker Ted MacDougall scored twice for United, but we were in great form that night and ended up thrashing them 5-2. I scored two, one coming from a volley that was hit so well it almost burst the net. Drew Jarvie, Ian Taylor and Barrie Mitchell got the other goals. George Best did not look all that interested – he had a history of turning off in friendlies – but he showed enough flashes of skill before being substituted to make the fans in the north-east believe they had got value for money. My abiding memory of George was the way in which wives and girlfriends swooned when he walked into the tearoom after the match. He spent as long as was required signing autographs and posing for pictures with fans outside Pittodrie. He did not refuse anyone, and acted as the perfect gentleman. I was fortunate to get to know George well later in life when we became regulars on the after-dinner speaking circuit. He remained the same, a man who made time for everyone and made audiences buzz by simply turning up. I didn't drink too often with George, for I doubt that I could have stood the pace, but it's a privilege to be able to say that I mixed with the man that I reckon was, without doubt, the greatest British (and of course Northern Irish) footballer.

That friendly v Manchester United was squeezed into a congested list of fixtures. We had to sandwich the first leg of our League Cup tie against Falkirk between the two European ties, and an amazing second-half display at home made the return trip to Brockville a waste of time. It was 0-0 at half-time, but we blew Falkirk away by scoring eight goals without reply within 38 minutes in the second period. I helped myself to a hat-trick, including one from the penalty-spot. Drew Jarvie popped in a couple and Jim Forrest, Arthur Graham and Davie Robb also got in on the act. I scored another two in the first half down at Brockville, which meant we were 10-0 ahead on aggregate and assured of a place in the quarter-finals. In the event we slackened off and allowed Falkirk to fight back and win the game 3-2.

We would probably have hit East Fife for eight were it not for an outstanding display from goalkeeper Dave Gorman at Pittodrie in the first leg of the quarter-finals. Ian Taylor, Drew and I finally beat him to make it 3-0 and ensure we would not have too much to worry about at Methil where I scored again as we ran out 4-1 winners to reach the last four by 7-1 on aggregate.

Once again Celtic stood in our path and our semi-final clash at Hampden proved controversial. I put Aberdeen ahead on the half-hour, but Celtic equalised within three minutes after being awarded a soft penalty which Harry Hood converted. We thought we were on the way to the final when Zoltan Varga fed a corner-kick to Davie Robb who cracked a header into goal to make the score 2-1 with 16 minutes left on the clock. Our fans were still celebrating when Jimmy Johnstone scored from a blatantly offside position and the goal was allowed to stand despite our strong protests. Celtic made it 3-2 with 10 minutes to go when Hood's pass was missed by Kenny Dalglish only for Tom Callaghan to smash the ball past Bobby Clark. Zoltan and I struck the woodwork with shots as we threw everything we had at Celtic, but they held out to set up a final with Eddie Turnbull's Hibs, which we would have loved to contest, for obvious reasons.

I took some consolation from the fact the Hibernian emerged

from the showdown as 2-1 winners to make up for being hammered 6-1 by Celtic in the Scottish Cup final the previous May. It was Hibs' first trophy win for 20 years, and it was great to see my old gaffer backing up my claim about him being the best in the business. We had come so close to beating Celtic, and I was determined to go one better when our Scottish Cup campaign got under way in the New Year. Our hopes of catching Celtic in the league were fading once more, especially after we drew 1-1 at Airdrie, who were eventually relegated. I didn't know it at the time, but the match on Saturday, 2 December 1972 was to be my last in an Aberdeen shirt for nearly four years.

11

THE PRIDE OF PLAYING FOR SCOTLAND

*'I was in a blind panic, especially
when I could not find a toilet'*

Gaining only four Scotland caps infuriates me to this day.
Playing for my country was a major high, and I'm convinced
that I was good enough to have appeared in far more international fixtures. A combination of bias because I was with a
provincial club, Aberdeen, and an unjust life-ban imposed on me
by the SFA – which I will explain in a later chapter – resulted in
my pulling on a dark blue shirt all too infrequently. Scotland
managers have denied any prejudice, but it is clear that footballers have more chance of gaining Scotland caps if they are
involved with the Old Firm or clubs in England. How else to
explain that I was constantly ignored by Scotland when I was
banging in so many goals for the Dons? If I had been wearing the
blue of Rangers or green and white of Celtic, you can be sure
that I would have been promoted in the reckoning.

The experience of my old pal Jimmy Bone around the time
that I was waiting and hoping for a Scotland chance highlighted
flaws in the selection process. Jimmy was a committed performer
who helped Partick Thistle to shock Celtic 4-1 in the 1971 Scottish
League Cup final, but he was not mentioned in dispatches for

Scotland until after he made a £30,000 switch to Norwich City early the following year. Suddenly he become a better prospect and was pushed ahead of me in the pecking order. Jimmy is a lovely man, but I reckon that I was the better striker, and I also reckon that his transformation into an Anglo-Scot resulted in him being the man that I replaced as a substitute when I finally gained my first cap against Denmark in Copenhagen in October of 1972.

Prejudice against players from the likes of Aberdeen, Dundee United and Hibernian is less of a factor these days, mainly because fewer Scots are involved with Rangers and Celtic and the top clubs in England. It is strange, though, that former Dundee United skipper Barry Robson and ex-Hibs midfielder Scott Brown became more regularly involved with Scotland after they had switched to Celtic. I would also argue that Kris Boyd was as deadly a striker when he was with Kilmarnock, and being ignored by Scotland, as he was when he had joined Rangers and become an international regular. Back in the 1970s Scotland managers seemed to be far more easily influenced by the media in the west of Scotland and, as I was to find out, by some of the big-name players they had to handle. I had dreamed of playing for Scotland since childhood, and the reader will recall that I was robbed of the chance at schoolboy level when my teacher withdrew me from the squad to face England after I had played in a bounce match with pals. I was more fortunate after signing for Morton and was chosen to play against England at Ibrox in early 1964. I scored and hoped that would be enough to earn me a place in the Scotland squad who were due to compete in the European Youth Championships finals in the Netherlands in March and April of that year.

I was most upset when I was overlooked, but I forced the selectors to reconsider when the Scotland youngsters, including future Leeds United star Peter Lorimer, lost 2-1 in a friendly against Morton's youth side. I landed the Morton goals in a two-minute period and newspaper stories maintained that it was a great mistake that I had not made the international squad. I was invited to a trial game at Dunfermline the following Monday, and I was ecstatic when I did enough to convince the selectors to include me in the pool of 16 heading for the finals. Also among those chosen was Henry McLeish, a future First Minister of Scotland.

The tournament is all but forgotten in Scotland despite our reaching the semi-finals and enjoying a memorable experience. At 16 I was the youngest member of a squad that included Bobby Clark, who was destined to be a team-mate and a close friend at Aberdeen, Wolves winger Paddy Buckley – son of the former Dons and Scotland player of the same name – Jim McCalliog of Chelsea, Bobby Watson of Rangers and Peter Lorimer.

We opened against Switzerland at Deventer, and I was over-joyed to score twice in a 3-1 victory. I was interviewed after the match for the *Daily Record* by the late Jim Rodger, and I said: 'I'm just a very lucky boy. My football heroes are Denis Law and Jim Baxter, and I want to be as famous as them some day.' That was not enough to keep me in the role of main striker for our next game, which was also versus Switzerland, this time in Amersfoort, as the curious format involved deciding these ties over two legs. I was moved to the right wing to make way for Lorimer, and we won 2-0 thanks to goals from Buckley and Hibs' Jim O'Rourke. This set up a quarter-final with Sweden and we beat them 1-0 at Amsterdam's Olympic Arena to proceed to a semi-final with Spain, which was scheduled for Den Bosch. It proved to be an epic battle in which we fought back from a goal down to lead 2-1 through strikes from O'Rourke and his Hibs team-mate Jim Stevenson. The Spaniards equalised before the interval and snatched the winner five minutes from time. In the final they lost 4-0 to England, and we were determined to end in the ascendancy by beating Portugal in the third/fourth play-off. I was delighted to score with Buckley as we fought back from 2-0 down. The Portuguese goalkeeper made an unbelievable save from my net-bound shot in the last couple of minutes to ensure extra-time, and they snatched the winner as we ran out of steam. We headed home satisfied with our efforts in finishing fourth in a tournament that had kicked off with 24 countries competing, and the trip prepared me for my first-team debut for Morton that summer, but unlike Lorimer and some of the others, no more Scotland youth caps came my way.

I had moved on to Huddersfield Town by the time my next Scotland chance came along, and that adventure included the fear of being kidnapped in Hong Kong. No caps were awarded as the tour of May and June 1967 was deemed unofficial by the SFA. Scotland had originally intended to send off a full squad, but the Old Firm and major clubs in England refused to release players, and that left no option but to name a touring squad made up mostly of young lads who were aided by a few experienced men, including my future Aberdeen manager Alex Ferguson, who was then a bustling striker with Dunfermline. I did not give it a thought at the time, but I wonder if that tour provided the catalyst for the difficult relationship that arose between Fergie and me at Pittodrie. He certainly made it clear from the moment the squad met up that he saw himself as top dog among the strikers, and he was planning to use the trip to enhance his chances of getting a full cap. He gave it a good go in scoring 10 goals in the seven games in which he played on tour, but I nipped in with eight in only two appearances to steal some of his thunder. Alex Ferguson did not graduate to full-cap status, and I can't help wondering if he bore some sort of grudge over my stealing the limelight at the end of a crazy seven-week trip.

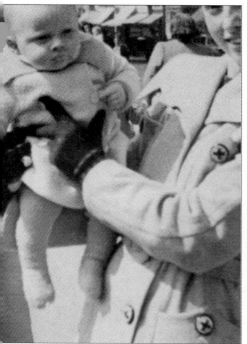

ABE IN ARMS: My mother shows me off to
[t]he world, aged just three months.

GROWING PAINS: My parents with me soon
afterwards ... note the fancy coat!

[H]ARBOUR HONEY: Doing my best 'Oor Wullie' impersonation down at the waterfront in
[G]reenock.

AYE READY: With a pal proudly dressed in my Boy's Brigade uniform.

DYANAMIC DUO: Posing with my dad, who has been my rock, at BB camp. Note the turn-up in the jeans!

SUPER SKIPPER: Holding the cup after helping my primary school to glory in 1960.

CHAMPIONS: I'm second left in the front row as Mount High School celebrate yet another cup triumph in 1962.

RISING STAR: I'm clearly happy during my early days at Morton. From the left, Ian Henderson, Billy Sinclair, me, Joe Lauchlan, Alec Byrne.

HATRICK HERO: Celebrating completing an early treble for Morton against Partick Thistle.

TALK OF THE TOWN: Posing for the camera after my move to Huddersfield Town.

WORLD TRAVELLER: With the Scotland squad that went on an epic tour in 1967. I'm in the centre of the front row. Alex Ferguson, my future boss, is fourth from the right in the back row.

JPER EDDIE: The boss, Eddie Turnbull, shows me how its done during training with Aberdeen.

TRIKE ONE: The first of my 205 goals for the Dons, from the spot against Partick Thistle in 1969.

FALSE DON: Training with Hungarian midfielder Zoltan Varga, left, and my old pal George Murray. I've never agreed with Varga being regarded as a Pittodrie legend.

BEST OF ENEMIES: My mate Jim Forrest, left, and big Willie Young help me get into shape with the Dons. Willie and I never got on and ended up brawling during a night out.

WAY DAY: On our way to get the train to Edinburgh to play Hibs in 1970. From left, Derek cKay, Henning Boel, Jim Forrest, Jim Hermiston, me, Jim Whyte.

N TARGET: Scoring for the Dons against Partick Thistle. The Jags must have been sick of the ght of me by then!

KING OF THE SWINGERS: The ball boy looks chuffed as I grapple with the net after scoring aga at Pittodrie.

GLORY GOAL: A rarely seen view of my spot kick in the 1970 Scottish Cup final, which I scored despite the efforts of the Celtic players to put me off.

CLINCHER: My great friend Derek McKay scored two in the final. Derek (No 7) slots his second home from a pass by me (No 10).

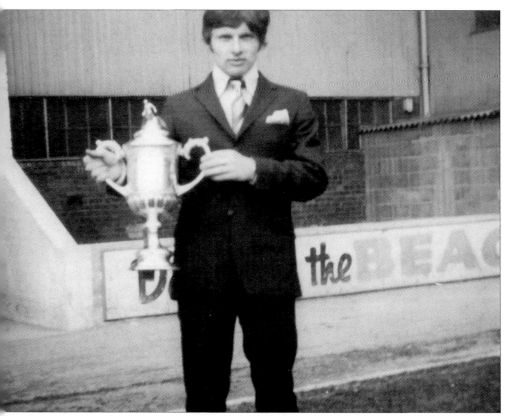

SILVER DARLING: One from my personal album as I pose with the Scottish Cup back at Pittodrie.

CHEERS: Boss Jimmy Bonthrone, Alec Willoughby and me celebrate beating Celtic again in the Drybrough Cup final at Pittodrie in 1971.

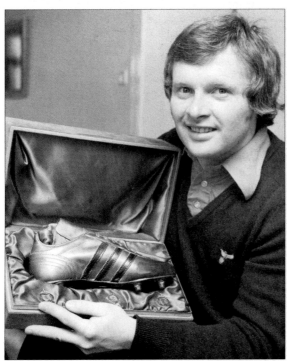

BOOT BOY: With my UEFA bronze boot for finishing the third top scorer in Europe in 1972.

EURO HERO: Future Scotland boss Berti Vogts looks on as I score against German side Borussia Munchengladbach in 1972. Berti had his revenge in the return match!

TOFFEE'S TOFF: I loved scoring this screamer for Everton against Leeds United at Elland Road.

STARR MAN: My friendship with comedian Freddie Starr was one of the major bonuses from my time as an Everton player.

BIG JOE, LITTLE JOE: Playing cards with Everton legend Joe Royle on the team bus to an away game in 1972.

HARPER OF HIBS: In action for the Hibees after failing to secure a dream move back to Pittodrie.

HEADLINE MAKER: Stories like this one about the Copenhagen Affair made me cringe because I knew Arthur Graham and I had done nothing wrong.

SUPER ALLY: The late, great, Ally MacLeod displays the League Cup to the delighted Dons fans from the balcony of Aberdeen's Town House in 1976 after our 2-1 victory over Celtic at Hampden.

ARGENTINA HERE WE COME: With room mates Derek Johnstone and Alan Rough on our way
to the 1978 World Cup finals.

WORKING HARD: Training in Cordoba. From left, Asa Hartford, boss Ally MacLeod, Sandy
Jardine, Kenny Burns, Alan Rough, me, Stuart Kennedy.

MY HEROES: With Morton legend Allan McGraw, the great Billy McNeill and a fan at a dinner i
the 1990s.

TRIBUTE TIME: Jimmy Bonthrone, me and Alex Ferguson with guests at my testimonial dinner. I
didn't know it at the time but Fergie had already decided my Dons days were over. The guy second
left in the back row looking like a surprised caveman is by best friend, Ally Kennedy.

BABY BOOM: Ex-wife Fiona and I greet Joanna's arrival along with Ross and Laura.

APPY FAMILIES: Here's me on holiday with the not so young kids in France in 2000. Joanna is ving her old man a cuddle, with Ross at the rear and Laura cosying up as well.

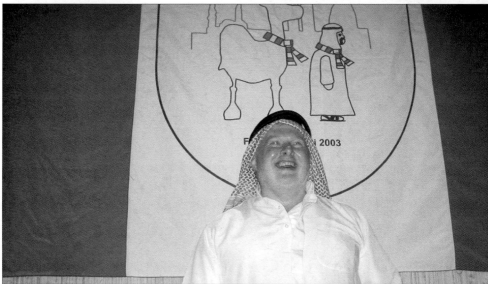

Top. HAT-TRICK: Ross, me, his partner Sarah and my beloved Shiela in fancy head gear during a holiday in Spain.

Above. SECRET SHEIKH: Here I am in disguise speaking at a Dons fans' dinner in Dubai, which had been organised by club sponsor, Jim Geddie.

Right. MEDIA MAN: Commentating on a Dons game for the radio at Ibrox.

We opened the tour in Israel with a 2-1 win, goals coming from Fergie and Willie Morgan, but I did not view the proceedings because I was ill in bed at the hotel suffering a bad reaction to injections administered before we flew from Scotland. Our next game was more than a week away in Hong Kong, so I had plenty of time to recover. It had been suggested that the Crown Colony was unsafe because China and Chairman Mao were stirring up protests directed against the United Kingdom which had led to some kidnappings, and it came as no surprise that two trucks manned by armed soldiers greeted us and escorted us to our hotel. The atmosphere was uneasy, and it became more so during a game in which I came on as a substitute. As night descended protesters in the hills around the stadium began to light bonfires and to chant slogans, creating a quite curious and eerie environment. Fergie got another two in a 4-1 victory, but the visit almost created a crisis after some younger lads, myself included, decided to seek out souvenirs at a little market near the hotel. We turned a corner and came face to face with hundreds of militant Mao supporters marching through the streets. Some spotted us and began to race in our direction, but we were too quick for them and retreated to the safety of the hotel. I still wonder whether we were but a few paces away from being caught up in an international incident, because surely a group of Scottish footballers would have been seen as highly-prized ransom material by kidnappers.

The tour moved on, safely, to Australia where three games were fitted into six days. Fergie got the only goal in a 1-0 win over our hosts in Sydney, and we also beat them 2-1 in Adelaide and 2-0 in Melbourne. I did not take part, but I was seeing parts of the world of which I could only dream when I was a kid growing up in Greenock. Next stop was New Zealand, and I was overcome with joy to put together a hat-trick when we beat them 7-2 in Wellington. The international fixture may have been classed as unofficial, but it was still a special experience to score three times for Scotland.

I did not feature in a 4-1 success over an Auckland Select or in the victory by the same margin over Vancouver All-Stars after we had completed a long flight to Canada, but the match against the Canadians in Winnipeg was the one in which I hammered home five goals in a 7-2 climax to the tour.

I was still a youngster, so I was aware that I would probably be obliged to wait before receiving more call-ups, but I thought that the goals harvested in Canada at least would have ensured that my wait was not too long. I was selected for two Under-23 internationals against Wales in 1970, one played at Pittodrie, and I was also included in Scottish League select sides, but it annoyed me that five years elapsed before Tommy Docherty gave me a crack at earning a full cap. I had scored 27 goals for the Dons in all competitions in 1970-71 despite my league drought in the wake of the Pittodrie fire, and had followed that with 42 in all games in the next campaign, which had been good enough to earn Europe's Bronze Boot. But no cap to go with it.

Rumour suggested that I would be called up in April 1972 for a friendly against Peru and for the Home International series against Northern Ireland, Wales and England. My heart sank when an interview with Tommy appeared in the *Evening Express* on 22 April 1972. When reporter Jimmy Forbes suggested that my record of 52 goals in my past 58 appearances for Aberdeen was impressive, Tommy replied: 'There is more to football than scoring 50 goals. I appreciate the Aberdeen fans may feel Harper has been slighted, but I don't look at it in that light.' The manager explained that he had picked Peter Lorimer, who had scored 27 goals for Leeds United the previous season, because he had achieved his total in a tougher league!

I was convinced that my chance of achieving a full Scotland cap had gone, so I was surprised to be informed at Pittodrie the following October that I had been included in Tommy's squad for a World Cup qualifier against Denmark in Copenhagen. I rushed home to tell my wife Fiona, and as soon as I arrived she informed me that she had some good news. 'So have I,' I said, but told her to go first. 'I'm pregnant,' she announced. The script could not have been more inspiring. To be told that fatherhood beckoned and to be named in the full Scotland squad at the same time was unbelievable. I was elated when I flew out with the squad the following Tuesday, but Tommy depressed my spirits after we had finished training in the Danish capital by taking me aside and saying: 'It's only fair to tell you Joe that you won't be playing tomorrow. I've watched you six or seven times, but have to say I've never been all that impressed. Others have watched you as well and told me that you have been playing well recently, hence why you are here. But I'm not sure you are good enough to play in a game as important as this one.'

I could not believe what I had heard. Those were hardly the inspiring words I had expected to come from the national manager . . . and I have never forgotten them. I admired Tommy for at least being man enough to tell me straight, but I was wondering whether I would be just as well returning to the hotel, packing my bags and departing on the next flight home. Then he baffled me by adding: 'What I can promise you, Joe, is that barring injury, you will play up front with Kenny Dalglish in the return game with Denmark at Hampden. What better way could there be to make your Scotland debut than at Hampden in front of your own people?' Within seconds Tommy Docherty had stabbed a dagger deep into my heart then sent it soaring with the most exciting news I had received in my football career: a promise that I would be playing for Scotland at long last. The thought of that outweighed other considerations, so I hid the disappointment of being left out in Copenhagen and con-centrated on helping the rest of the lads to prepare for kick-off.

I was in for another surprise, though, when Tommy named the team and substitutes, with mine coming last in line. I was so stunned that I turned to Lou Macari and inquired: 'Is there another Harper with us over here?' Lou responded with a laugh: 'If there was, you would be at home.' I would at least be in a Scotland strip for a full international for the first time that night.

Tommy had said that I definitely would not play, so I continued doing my bit to get the lads prepared and went so far as to administer some leg massages. It was a thrill at least to be on the bench as Scotland's followers, who had helped to pack the stadium to its 31,000 capacity, cheered us on with their familiar fervour. With about half an hour of the tie remaining the manager shouted down the line of substitutes: 'Get ready, you're going on.' I had to ask if he really meant me, and a nod of Tommy's head confirmed the order. I was off the bench like a bullet and began to take off my tracksuit for a warm-up, which I planned to make one of the shortest in Scottish football history because I was so desperate to get on the pitch. I was horrified to be distracted suddenly by an overwhelming desire to visit the toilet. The manager could see I had stopped in my tracks and the intimate conversation went like this:

'*Hurry up, I want you on now.*'
'*I can't, gaffer.*'
'*Why not?*' (Delivered with agitation).
'*Because I need to pee.*'
(It seemed the manager did not know whether to laugh or hit me).
'*Well go and bloody do it, but hurry up.*'
(Manager turned away, shaking head).

As I raced up the tunnel I could not believe what was happening to me. I had spent most of my life dreaming of playing for Scotland, and now that I was on the brink of doing so I had been let down by a weak bladder. When I look back I realise the situation was farcical and can laugh about it. But I was in a blind panic, especially when I could not find a toilet. I inquired of two policemen, who pointed me in the direction of two big iron doors. I was desperate, so I barged through them – and discovered I was outside the stadium. The doors slammed shut behind me. My main priority was to relieve myself, which I did there and then, but I couldn't help wondering if my Scotland dreams were heading down the drain too. I was trembling with panic because I was locked out, though now and then I could spot the ball as it was kicked high in the air above the stadium. I banged on the door and shouted: 'Let me in', hoping that the two policemen would come to my rescue. It seemed like an eternity before the doors were reopened, but the policemen treated me as a frantic fan – I was still wearing my tracksuit – and attempted to direct me through a turnstile to the stand. They let me proceed after I showed them I was wearing kit beneath the tracksuit and I pleaded that I was a Scotland player. By the time I got back down the tunnel, I was worried that Tommy might have decided to put someone else on. He just shook his head in disbelief once more, told me to forget the warm-up and put me straight on as a replacement for Jimmy Bone.

That would have been good enough for me, but my debut proved to be what dreams are made of when I latched onto a clever back-heel from wee Lou Macari to score Scotland's fourth as we won 4-1. It was hard to take it all in. I had gone from the high of being told I was going on to the low of fearing that I would become the first Scotland player to miss his debut because he had needed the toilet, then finished by scoring in my first appearance. I could not have been happier when I returned to Scotland to celebrate with family and friends, and the joy intensified when Tommy was true to his word and picked me from the start for the return match versus the Danes on November 15, 1972. We again emerged as victors, by 2-0, with Peter Lorimer and Kenny Dalglish scoring. It was a big thrill to represent my country at Hampden alongside the great Kenny, a footballing genius who in my opinion takes his place in the top three of Scotland greats with Denis Law and Billy Bremner. Kenny displayed superb technique and the quickest of football brains, and I am still aggrieved at not fully realising just how quick. He looked to be going nowhere at Hampden when surrounded by Danish defenders, so I stopped making the sort of run on which I would normally set off in the hope of meeting a cross. Kenny twisted and turned to create space and duly sent in a magnificent cross, but by the time I had switched on to what he had done I was too late, and I could not connect as the ball sped past me with the Danish goal gaping a few inches away.

I vowed not to let that happen the next time I got the chance to play alongside Kenny, because I was convinced that recording a goal and victories in my first two appearances would boost my claims for further caps. I was wrong. Tommy Docherty moved on to manage Manchester United just as I was starting my spell at Everton. His successor Willie Ormond, who had served as manager of St Johnstone, was familiar with my capabilities and named me in a few provisional squads, but I did not progress to the final selections. He also named me in the original list of 30 players for the 1974 World Cup finals in Germany, but I was forced to withdraw because I had suffered a knee injury. I was, however, presented with one of the Vauxhall Vivas offered to players who appeared in the finals or qualifiers.

Willie Ormond was fairly weak as a manager and I felt he was influenced far too much by the press, who seemed to be more in favour of Lou Macari, Colin Stein or even Derek Parlane rather than Joe Harper backing up Joe Jordan and Dalglish. He also found it difficult to exert authority over some of the senior squad members, Billy Bremner, in particular. That was confirmed when I was playing cards with a few lads in Billy's room while attending a training camp at Largs. Willie wandered in clad in his pyjamas and suggested politely to Billy that it was getting late and it was time to shut the card school. Billy's response was poetic: 'Now Willie Winkie, away you back to your bed and I will decide when we are ready to go to ours.' I was rather shocked to witness the Scotland captain speak to the manager like that, but Willie accepted the admonition and departed in his nightgown. To be fair to Billy, he had to provide much of the motivational chat before international matches because Willie did not do much of that.

It was almost three years after making my debut before I got the chance to claim the third of my four caps. It took me back to Copenhagen, but a fairytale ending of the Hans Christian Andersen variety was not in store this time.

12

EVERTON COME CALLING

'I have always felt guilty about the departure'

I still get angry deep down whenever I recall the disgraceful way in which Aberdeen FC treated their fans when I was sold to Everton in 1972. I believe they conned the supporters by keeping them in the dark about what was going on. There is no other way to describe it.

Let me explain for the first time the details of what happened when Everton stunned the Dons' directors by offering £180,000, a record fee between two British clubs, for my services. I had been capped by Scotland, I was on a professional high and I was looking forward to banging in more goals for Aberdeen to remain in the international limelight. The move by Everton came out of the blue. I was selecting a Christmas tree for the house at a forest on the outskirts of the city (and in the Aberdonian tradition of doing so without permission) when the clubs began negotiations via the telephone on the evening of Friday, 9 December 1972. When a pal and I returned to the house, we discovered the tree we had chosen illicitly was too tall to stand upright in the living-room. Serves us right. As we headed for the door my wife Fiona mentioned that Dons boss Jimmy Bonthrone had phoned, and I had to make contact with him as soon as possible. I told her I would get round to it when we had come back with a tree that was more suitable. My pal and I were off again driving through the streets with the rejected tree sticking out the back of my car. We had measured the size required this time and had just finished gingerly fitting the new tree into the car when we spotted torches flashing through the forest in our direction. A voice shouted: 'Stop, Forestry Commission' and a whistle sounded, which prompted us to jump into the car and scarper. I know such conduct was stupid. If we had been caught, my position as a leading Dons player would have guaranteed blaring headlines, but I was about to make the newspapers in a big way for professional reasons.

It was late at night when Fiona asked me if I had phoned Jimmy back. We were due to face Arbroath at home in the league the next day, so I told her that I would catch up with him when the squad met at lunchtime. I changed my mind when Fiona said Jimmy had insisted it was important that I called him that night, and the first thing he said when I phoned was: 'Where have you been?' He sounded in a bit of a panic and I feared there might be some bad news coming, but he explained: 'There's a move on. You have to meet me earlier tomorrow.' I inquired: 'A move to where? He said that he could not tell me until the following day, which did not go down well with me. All that Jimmy would reveal was that a big move was in the offing, one that would be good for me and Aberdeen. 'But I don't want to leave,' I protested.

To be sure, some debate had arisen in recent weeks about my future, mainly because I had stated in an interview with the *Evening Express* that I would stay with Aberdeen only if the club showed that they retained the ambition to win cups and titles. I had also declared a desire eventually to return to the English game, but my main target at that point without doubt was to claim a league-winners' medal with the Dons, especially after having gone so close in recent seasons. I was hoping that Aberdeen would be able to convince me they were just as hungry as I was, and I would have been delighted to stay at Pittodrie for a while. Matters seemed to have been taken out of my hands, and I was not willing to co-operate if Jimmy would not reveal the identity of the club that wanted my services. 'Stuff your meeting!' I said, adding that I was about to hang up and would meet up with the rest of lads as normal the next day. Jimmy became more flustered and told me that he would reveal the team's identity only if I promised not to tell anyone. It was a laughable situation, but I simply had to know, so I agreed to the gagging order. '*Everton* want to sign you,' the manager confided. 'You have to speak to them tomorrow. I will pick you up at 7 a.m.' I asked about the game against Arbroath, but he told me not to worry about that and hung up.

My wife obviously wanted to know which team had come in for me, and I told her the name. 'Where's Everton?' she asked. I could not enlighten her, and we had to check the fact that Everton belong to Liverpool. Remember that those were the days long before blanket coverage of English football was on offer on television, which has helped to instil in many fans an encyclopedic knowledge of clubs in the Premier League. I had heard of Everton, of course, but had not needed to find out where their stadium was situated. More homework that night confirmed that if the deal was sealed, I would be joining one of the biggest clubs in English football. 'The biggest problem is I really don't want to leave Aberdeen,' I told Fiona.

I spent a sleepless night and negative experiences of Huddersfield were uppermost in my mind when I dragged myself into Jimmy Bonthrone's car just before 7 a.m. on Saturday. We changed cars at Stonehaven, and Jimmy, club chairman Dick Donald and I sped to Glasgow to meet the Everton delegation at the Excelsior Hotel. 'I really don't want to leave, Mr Chairman,'

I exclaimed, using the respectful mode of address that was reserved for Dick Donald at Pittodrie. 'You have to, Joe,' he emphasised. 'The offer is too good for us to turn down, and I'm sure you will be well looked after as well.' I was informed in Glasgow that the clubs had settled the deal in my absence, and it was merely a matter of sorting out personal details. One stumbling block arose because Aberdeen had arranged an interest-free loan of £2,000 towards the house that Fiona and I had just bought. It would have to be repaid, and I asked the chairman if he would write off the loan given that I had done well for the club and they were about to rake in a fee of £180,000. He refused, so I told him that the transfer was off, proclaiming: 'I've never asked to go, anyway. I'm happy at Pittodrie. In fact, why don't we get back up the road and sort out an extended contract, and we can forget any of this happened?' I was serious, but Dick Donald's expression confirmed that he was not pleased, and he responded with: 'You are leaving, and that's the end of it.'

Everton's manager Harry Catterick stepped in to assist the process. He had already done a great job of selling his club and in convincing me that he would be a great boss to play for, and he asked to speak to me in private once more. I mentioned the problem of the £2,000 loan. 'It's clear that we really want you, and Aberdeen are happy for you to leave,' said Harry. 'We will pay you the £2,000 on top of what we have already agreed. Go back and ask them if they will take £1,000. If they do, you can keep the rest and treat it as a gift from us.' I did just that. Dick agreed to accept a £1,000 repayment, shook my hand and performed a little jig to which he was prone when happy. It was still only 11 a.m., and the deal was done. I was an Everton player, had arranged an unexpected bonus into the bargain, and I naturally anticipated heading back to Aberdeen to say farewell to my team-mates and perhaps to wave goodbye to the Dons fans at the Arbroath game. 'No you won't,' Dick stressed. 'And I don't want you telling any journalist about the transfer. We will deal with that.'

That was that. I was packed into a car with Harry and other Everton officials and was on my way to Liverpool, but Aberdeen's next move caused me anger and upset. The board could have released news of the transfer to Dons fans before the Arbroath game via press, radio or television, but decided not to do so. The powers that be waited until Aberdeen supporters were in the ground and informed them of my departure over the loudspeakers as the team-sheets were being read out! Shocking and thoughtless, to my mind, and the supporters made their feelings clear by booing and jeering the directors throughout the game. Several Dons fans that I have met over the years told me that they had walked out in disgust at the disrespectful way they had been treated that day late in 1972 – and they did not return until I had rejoined the club in 1976. I had nothing to do with what happened or the way in which matters were handled; I was in Liverpool being prepared for a welcoming press conference that Everton had organised. But I have always felt guilty about the departure because I adore the Aberdeen fans and the last thing I would wish to do is upset any of them. My guilt feelings became more intense when I learned that the Dons had drawn 0-0, which saw them slip to fifth spot in the league six points behind Celtic, who also had a game in hand. It was clear that league glory was again unlikely to be realised by the Dons that season, but I had a new set of problems to confront.

Fiona and I were wary about setting up house in Liverpool, mainly because she was pregnant and wanted to be near her family in Glasgow. It was a great opportunity for us, though, so we vowed to make the best of it.

Everton booked us into a pleasant hotel and a strange incident took place during our first night. The phone rang and a male caller asked if I would meet him at a bus stop across the street from the hotel. 'I'm from Everton,' he announced. I was a bit apprehensive, especially on a dull night with poor visibility and heavy rain, but I made my way to meet the mysterious man. He was wearing a long raincoat and reached inside to produce a bulging sealed brown envelope which he handed over. 'That's for the baby,' he said. 'You will never see me again,' He wandered off into the rain, mirroring a scene from a black-and-white mystery movie, and I never did see him again. When I got back to the hotel room Fiona and I opened the envelope to discover £2,000 made up of crisp new £20 notes. My wife was perturbed and suggested that I should hand it back, but to whom? It was obviously the extra money that I had negotiated from the transfer deal, so after a fair bit of persuading Fiona agreed that we should keep it, especially when we would soon have an extra mouth to feed. Thus began the next stage of my career, which would be brightened considerably by striking up a friendship with one of Britain's funniest men.

13

FLYING FUN WITH FREDDIE STARR

❖

'It is a good day to die for the emperor!'

I was at my best for my debut for Everton against Tottenham Hotspur at Goodison Park on 16 December 1972. I missed a penalty, but apart from that it was one of those days when everything I tried came off. I sprayed 40-yard passes, many of them half-volleys, straight to the feet of team-mates, won every tackle and header and set up two goals for Howard Kendall. I also struck shots against the Spurs bar twice and hit both posts.

I was desperate to cap things with a goal, so I was delighted when we were awarded a penalty in the closing minutes. I executed a slight shuffle on the run-up which sent Spurs keeper Pat Jennings the wrong way, but to my horror I blasted the ball high and wide of the other post. We won 3-1, though, and I felt on top of the world when the Everton fans gave me a standing ovation and chanted my name at the conclusion. I was still on cloud nine when I met a pal, John Low, owner of the prize-winning Ashvale Chip Shop in Aberdeen. He and his wife were guests at the game, and we were having cups of tea in the players' lounge when one of the Everton lads asked if I would be willing to meet their No. 1 celebrity fan. That was Freddie Starr, the top comedian who had me in stitches when I watched his antics on TV.

Freddie gave me a hug and said he was excited to meet me, but the excitement was all mine because he was the celebrity. Freddie is Everton-daft, and he insisted that John and I and our wives accept an invitation to attend his stage show that night at Liverpool's Wooky Hollow nightclub.

He took us to his house where we met his wife Betty, one of the most down-to-earth and warm-hearted of people. Their mansion was massive and tastefully decorated, but they had no airs and graces. While Betty went to cook some steaks Freddie poured the drinks, but pointed out that he would abstain because he was working that night. Betty shouted that the steaks were ready and I expected to be ushered into a fancy dining-room, but she returned with a tray stacked with steaks in big rolls: she and Freddie preferred steak butties eaten off their laps, an example of how untouched they were by the wealth his success had brought.

We were ushered to the best seats at his show later on, and I admit that I felt a wee bit embarrassed when the star came on stage for a comedy sketch wearing an Everton shirt with the name Harper and No. 9 displayed on the back. Freddie taunted Liverpool fans in the audience – their team had lost that day – by presenting a commentary of how well I had done at Goodison on my debut, including mimicking my array of passes and shots that had struck woodwork. He finished by lining up to take a penalty in front of a wee set of five-a-side goals set out on stage . . . then blasted the ball at the Liverpool fans. 'And that's how wide of the mark the wee fat bastard was with his penalty, as well,' Freddie shouted, and the audience roared with laughter. Freddie and Betty became close friends of ours, and Fiona and I stayed at their house for the first three months of my spell with Everton. Betty knew that Fiona was pregnant, and she brushed away our protests when we insisted that the hotel Everton had arranged was good enough.

I have always been grateful for the kindness that our new friends showed, though life with Freddie is a rollercoaster ride because he is as mad off the stage as on it. I recall him entering the lounge on a Sunday morning – he was a late riser because usually he had been appearing in Blackpool the previous night. He was wearing a dressing-gown and looking at us in his usual mischievous way. He opened the curtains with the electric control, then stood at the window and opened the dressing-gown wide to reveal a giant fake penis with flashing lights adorning the end, which was strapped around his waist. Old ladies who were passing by on their way church were suitably startled. You had to be prepared at all times for a wind-up.

Freddie loved to play table football, and was suitably attired in England kit. After scoring a goal he would race into the garden and embark on laps of honour shouting 'goooooaaaaallllll!' at the top of his voice. That happened after each score, and our games often lasted for hours of fun. Being football-crazy, he had two small goals set up in his back garden, and the two of us would play Scotland v England games every Sunday. Even in bad weather our host insisted on playing, so we were often covered from head to toe in mud by the end. Muddy or not, Freddie insisting one day that we drive to the local shop in his white Rolls-Royce, which also featured a beautiful white-furred interior, to buy ice-cream. The interior was transformed into a terrible state, and staff were treated to the weird sight of a mud-spattered Freddie wandering in to order ice-creams by means of a marvellous impression of film star John Wayne.

Freddie's generosity was emphasised when we mentioned that we had been obliged to turn down an invitation to a Highland ball organised by Fiona's sister Maggie in Glasgow, because Everton were playing a home game on the day, and we would find it hard to reach Scotland in time. 'Forget that,' said Freddie. 'You and Fiona make sure you are ready right after the game, and I will get my driver to pick you up.' We could not refuse, though we assumed we would be driving to Glasgow amid the luxury of Freddie's Rolls-Royce. However, his driver delivered us onto the tarmac at Liverpool Speke Airport, where Freddie was standing beside a six-seater aircraft. 'Hop in. Have you up in Glasgow in no time,' he assured us, before clambering in the front beside the pilot. Fiona and I sat behind them, and the rear seats were reserved for our golden retriever puppy, Rabbie.

Freddie had mentioned taking flying lessons, and we were airborne before I realised that the aircraft was fitted with two sets of controls. We were supplied with headsets, Freddie explaining that he was due to take more lessons and that his instructor had agreed that flying us to Glasgow would be ideal practice. The weather became a bit overcast and it started to rain as we approached our destination, so Fiona and I stared at each other in horror when we heard the instructor tell Freddie to get ready to land the plane. Freddie interjected: 'I've never landed it before. I'm not so sure I could do it in weather as bad as this, either.' But the instructor was adamant and indicated that Freddie should take charge: 'If you can land it in this weather, you will be able to land it in anything,' he said, reassuringly. We were shaking with fear, but, undaunted, Freddie reached beneath his seat and produced a kamikaze-style pilot's helmet which he put on. He also donned a gigantic pair of joke spectacles with lenses akin to bottle bottoms, and he began to babble in a mock Japanese accent. One line I recall with horror as the plane headed towards the runway was: 'It is a good day to die for the emperor!' Fiona and I kept our eyes shut tight and prayed for deliverance. The plane touched down without mishap, the cuddled-up and snoozing Rabbie blissfully unaware of the drama that had unfolded, and only then did Freddie reveal that the instructor had been in charge all the way from Liverpool, after all. Phew!

Freddie was performing in Blackpool that night, and he declined the offer to join us for a night out in Glasgow. The plane was refuelled and he set off on the return flight within 20 minutes, which meant that our trip back was rather less frightening, if more time-consuming. I had to be back in Liverpool by 9 a.m. on the Monday, so Fiona, Rabbie and I caught the mail train that left Queen Street Station, Glasgow, at three in the morning. The ancient carriage lacked heating, but we had borrowed a large rug from Fiona's sister and huddled under it with the dog for the four-hour journey. Slow going it might have been, but at least no mad kamikazes were threatening the railway.

Friendship with Freddy and Betty was a most pleasant diversion as I began to adjust to life as an Everton employee, and I loved spending time with them. It saddens me to this day that we lost touch when my unfolding career took me back to Scotland, and it was a real shame that they divorced some years later. I was excited to discover that Freddie had agreed to appear in the television programme *Celebrity Wife Swap* in 2007 with his new spouse. I tuned in and was not surprised that he received some bad press because he came over as a bit grumpy. I knew from the way he was behaving that he was purely acting up for the cameras, for he is a master of that craft. I hope that we will meet again: Freddie is a wonderful person and great fun.

At Everton I had to get used to the fact that we visited Goodison Park only when a home game was on the fixture-list; we trained at Bellfield and stepped inside our home ground about once a fortnight. At Aberdeen I had changed at Pittodrie for training and we had exercised in the car park across the road or at Seaton Park, where we might have to run around members of the public picnicking or out for a stroll. In winter when snow and ice were particularly bad it was a case of waiting for the tide to recede into the North Sea, so that we could use Aberdeen's beach to go through our paces. Not ideal in any way, and it's sad that almost 40 years since I joined up at Pittodrie that the Dons are still behind the times in not enjoying proper training facilities.

Settling in on Merseyside was made easier because Everton already had a couple of Scots on board in left-winger John Connolly and full-back John McLaughlin. We formed a cabaret act known as The Three Jocks to entertain workmates at the club's Christmas party. We dressed in kilts with giant sporrans and big floppy 'See you Jimmy' hats and sang daft Scottish songs, told jokes and performed a wee bit of Highland dancing. It went down well and helped me to become accepted quickly by the players, stars and all.

Among the most brilliant was Howard Kendall, who was among the best footballers that I was cast alongside. Howard was a genius when he was on the ball, but pretty quiet off the pitch. He was highly professional and focused on preparing properly, so I did not have the pleasure of socialising with him too often. Howard was a big hero with the Everton fans and I knew that I would score goals when he was about. The main target-man at the time was Joe Royle, but it is frustrating for me that he was plagued by injuries and so we did not get many opportunities to operate together. The rare combination of Little Joe and Big Joe did work well, so it's a real shame that a long-term partnership did not develop.

Manager Harry Catterick was a gentleman and I did not witness him losing his cool, even with a striker called Bernie Wright, who had a bit of a drink problem. Bernie was clearly a bit worse for wear one day and was ranting and raving at Harry at the training ground, and he was chasing him about because he was upset at being dropped. Harry did not respond, as many managers might have, but merely smiled and indicated that other players should usher Bernie away. It was sad to see how drink affected Bernie at times, though I must confess that his habit allowed some of us to play a prank on him that backfired. We were enjoying a team night out when Bernie got particularly drunk, so much so that as we were walking to a nightclub he lay down on the pavement and fell asleep. What were we to do with him? Well, we lifted him onto the back of a lorry that was parked nearby and covered him up with a bit of tarpaulin, planning to return to his aid once we had enjoyed a few more drinks. When we left the nightclub an hour or so later, however, the lorry and Bernie had vanished. He was raging the next day because he did not stir until the truck had reached Leeds, and he had to pay for a train ticket back to Liverpool.

Bernie made 11 appearances for Everton before his contract was terminated 'for serious misconduct' a few days after that training-ground spat with the manager. He eventually sorted himself out and was transformed into a big hero back at Walsall, the club he had left to join Everton, and he also turned out for Bradford and Port Vale.

My first goal for Everton came in a 1-1 draw with Chelsea at Stamford Bridge on 23 December 1972, and it was great to get off the mark against one of the biggest clubs in England. I recall that Stamford Bridge was being refurbished, so we were obliged to change in temporary huts which were set up behind one of the stands. I was in a hurry to catch a flight from London to Glasgow to deliver Christmas presents, and I rushed off the pitch to shower. I thought it was a nice touch by the host club to leave small bars of soap on the shower floor, and duly rubbed one all over my sweaty form, but failed to raise a lather. I merely rinsed off the mud, dried myself and headed for the airport – and soon detected a burning sensation on my skin. When I reached Glasgow I felt as if I had spent far too long sun bathing, and when I removed my shirt and checked in a mirror I found that my chest, stomach and legs were streaked red, and apart from the burning sensation my body was itching like mad. I eventually discovered that the bars of 'soap' left in the showers were actually those pungent chemical tablets which are used to ward off germs in public toilets. My defence, your honour: I had not set eyes on them before that first trip to London.

I added another goal the following Tuesday when we also drew 1-1 at home to Birmingham. I was on the score-sheet when we dumped Aston Villa out of the FA Cup by 3-2 in a thriller at Goodison Park, but dreams of Wembley were dashed when Millwall shocked us 2-0 at home in the next round. The highlight of that season was experiencing my first taste of a Merseyside derby v Liverpool at Goodison. We lost 2-0, but I must say that the atmosphere of the occasion was incredible. Many Scots claim that the Glasgow derby involving Rangers and Celtic is the best club game in the world, but I disagree strongly. Old Firm games harbour an ugly side because the atmosphere is tainted by religious bigotry that has led to people being murdered in the aftermath of some tussles. The Merseyside version is so much more appealing because, while it can divide families at times, lots of humour is involved amid the rivalry, and respect as opposed to hatred exists between the two camps. The games are just as competitive as the Old Firm versions, though I would argue that they reflect a higher standard simply because the quality of players at the top level in England tends to be superior.

I found out just how competitive in that initial clash with Liverpool. Larry Lloyd, their strapping centre-back, went over the top with his first tackle on me. I was fortunate to see it coming and was able to ride the challenge a little, because it had the potential to be a leg-breaker. I still required treatment and Larry leaned over and advised me: 'Listen son, when you play down here you play with men.' Minutes later Larry was rolling about in agony on the turf because one of my elbows accidentally collided with his face after we had tangled on the ground. Liverpool captain Emlyn Hughes rushed in to have a go at me, so I swung a right hook and caught him on the end of his nose, which gushed with blood. Players from both teams were now having a go at each other, and I expected to be sent off for an early bath. To my relief, the referee had missed my contribution and I was merely lectured about trying to keep my cool. Everton fans had spotted my reaction, though, and were clearly pleased that I had given Hughes his come-uppance. They cheered and applauded every time I got the ball, and Everton followers have told me that I was elevated to the status of legend after that incident. Lashing out at Emlyn was not what I would have wished to do, but I had learned quickly that if I wanted to survive in England I would have to convince defenders that they should not mess with me.

Some of football's genuine hardmen were about at the time, including Leeds United duo Norman Hunter and Billy Bremner, Chelsea's Ron 'Chopper' Harris and Liverpool's assassin Tommy Smith, who made Rangers captain John Greig seem like a pussycat by comparison. It was a case of get your retaliation in first with that lot, and I reckon I dished out as much punishment as I received. Not all the defenders down south were brutes. I was honoured to rejoin battle with the great Bobby Moore; I had faced up to him briefly in a cup-tie when with Huddersfield Town. Bobby was majestic and it was obvious why he was such an important element in England's 1966 World Cup-winning side. He had an uncanny knack of prising open the opposition with accurate defence-splitting passes and in almost every tackle he went in clean and fair. He was the finest defender that I faced by some distance, and a thoroughly pleasant character.

Events off the pitch meant that my thoughts of being a hero among the Everton fans over a prolonged period were shattered.

Fiona suffered severe health problems during and after the birth of our son Ross and made it clear that she would rather we returned to Scotland to be closer to her mother and the rest of the family, and Harry Catterick was forced to step down as manager, also because of ill-health. He had suffered a heart attack in January 1972, and his doctor decided that he could not continue in a job as stressful as football management. It was clearly difficult for Harry to step down for he had been a leading player with the club, and as manager had led the Toffees to two league titles and an FA Cup triumph in his 12 year spell in charge.

In April 1973 he took up a role as a director, his departure from the manager's office proving a massive blow for Everton. It was no surprise to see him move back into management with Preston North End a couple of years later, and I was very sad to learn of his death in 1985 at the age of 65. He suffered another heart attack while watching his beloved Everton playing Ipswich Town in an FA Cup-tie at Goodison. An Everton legend in life and death. Tommy Eggleston, who had managed Mansfield Town, took over as caretaker boss for a month or so in succession to Harry until the Everton directors secured a permanent replacement, and they settled on Billy Bingham, the renowned Northern Ireland international winger.

Many speak with great affection about the times they played under Billy, most notably former Northern Ireland and Manchester United defender Jimmy Nicholl, an individual I have got to know quite well since he became part of the management team at Aberdeen. But Billy and I just did not get on, and I'm convinced that he simply had something against Scottish players because he soon got rid of my pals John Connolly and a John McLaughlin. I suspected my days at Goodison Park were numbered too when the manager made a point of picking up on anything I did wrong, no matter how slight, almost from the day he arrived. It was disappointing because I had finished as

Everton's top-scorer at the end of my first season, with eight goals in 22 appearances. Billy made clear that he would build his own team and that many of Harry's signings would be getting the boot, which hardly boosted morale. He spoke of signing Bob Latchford, who had been starring for West Bromwich Albion, and the thought of competing with him and Joe Royle for a starting place raised my excitement level. But the word was that Billy wanted Latchford to replace me, which is what happened in the end.

My relationship with Billy worsened when we travelled to Norway on a pre-season tour in the summer of 1973. Mick Bernard, Roger Kenyon and I decided to visit a restaurant, but it was busy and service was slow and we were in danger of missing the 11 p.m. curfew imposed on us to ensure we returned to the hotel. We spotted an Everton director and explained our problem; he agreed that we should finish our meal and he undertook to sort it out with the manager. We ate as fast as we could and were directed to a shortcut back to the hotel, but that proved a wild-goose chase that took us to the rear of the building, and by the time we had made it to the entrance we were just under 10 minutes late. Billy immediately laid into us and fined us £100 each, ignoring the explanation about the club director having seen us. The disciplinary measures did not go down well with other players in the squad, who thought that Billy had been harsh, and our anger intensified when we got calls from home telling us that the incident had been splashed over the papers in Liverpool, with Billy quoted as saying we had been punished for trying to sneak in the back door of the hotel after returning back late from a drinking session. The amount of information included suggested that the story had been leaked by someone present at the meeting Billy had with us, and it certainly did not come from any of the footballers.

I tried continuing to convince Billy Bingham that I was the

man he should trust to get goals for Everton. I scored in his initial competitive game in charge, a 3-1 defeat at Leeds United, and I netted when he recorded his first win, a 3-0 hammering of Ipswich Town at Goodison, but I could tell that he was not impressed. That was disappointing, as I scored 17 times in my two half-seasons there, which I saw as a reasonable return from a player getting used to life in England's top division. Billy started relegating me to the reserves, and that combined with Fiona's poor health prompted the wish to return to Pittodrie. Billy was not pleased when I said as much in an interview with journalist Frank Gilfeather for the *Evening Express* in November 1973.

'If I got the chance to return to Pittodrie, I would jump at it,' I told Frank, who is now a fellow columnist for the Aberdeen-based newspaper. My heart soared when Billy interrupted a five-a-side game in which I was involved during training in February 1974 to tell me that Aberdeen wanted me back.

The year of 1973 was certainly an eventful one for me, not least because of the birth of our first child Ross on June 17. One reason that Fiona was keen to be close to her family was a bowel ailment which has plagued her for most of her adult life. It obviously got her down, but she is not one to complain, and I have always admired the way she handled the problem and the bravery that she showed in defying doctors who advised that she should not have more children after our son was born. We had made a point of being back in Glasgow for Ross's arrival, for we did not wish to have an Englishman in the Harper clan! I was at the hospital waiting for Ross to make his arrival when a doctor suggested that I should head home and rest. 'Come back in about two hours, and you will be right on time for the birth,' I was told. His forecast was spot-on, and when I returned to the hospital Ross was in the process of making his entrance to the world. I stood fascinated watching his birth, an experience that was more thrilling and exciting than any in my football career. I did not cope too well with the sight of blood, but that was nothing compared to how Fiona must have been feeling, and after Ross had been born a nurse arrived with a cup of tea and some toast which I accepted gratefully and started to consume. I was slightly embarrassed when the nurse pointed out that the refreshments were actually meant for the new mum.

We decided to hold a party at our house to celebrate Ross's arrival, and were disappointed when Freddie Starr said that he could not join us because he was working in Blackpool on the night. The celebrations were in full swing when a knock came to the door, and to our delight that announced Freddie's arrival. His driver kept the engine of the white Rolls-Royce ticking over while he did the rounds of members of our families and other guests, having whispered: 'I can only stay a few minutes.' He was present for about 10 minutes, cracking jokes in his inimitable style, then he shook my hand, kissed Fiona and left for his engagement. It was then that I realised he had not even mentioned the birth of our son, but as I pondered Freddie came back in and went up to Fiona to declare: 'By the way, I love your new monkey!' The star guest beat a swift retreat before the proud mum had a chance to throw him out.

Still on family matters, our daughter Laura was born on 4 June 1975, by which time I had moved to Hibernian and we were living in Glasgow. The doctor who had been on duty for Ross's birth was present once more – I had resolved to attend the births of all my children – and this time he told me to come back to the hospital in three hours' time. I got stuck in traffic, and missed Laura's arrival by about 30 seconds. Second daughter Joanna, who was born on 26 October 1977, is the family's true

Aberdonian, because I had returned to Pittodrie before her arrival, which was anything but plain sailing. Fiona needed an epidural injection to help with the pain of the lengthy labour and the midwife skelped Joanna on the backside after she had finally made her entrance, but there was no reaction. Another smack, still no response, and I was in a panic as medical staff removed wee Joanna for emergency treatment. To our great relief they returned almost immediately, and the baby proved that she had a healthy pair of lungs by screaming for some 45 minutes. We were told that the medication from the injection had passed into Joanna and that she had not been in any danger, but it was a scary experience.

Considering the medical advice that Fiona had been given after the birth of Ross, our daughters are living testimony to their mother's courage. The fact that my marriage to Fiona eventually ended does not detract from my admiration for her, nor from my utmost pride in becoming a father three times over.

14

HIBS' HATEFUL MOB

'I have no peace of mind, and I'm sure
the chairman doesn't like me'

It was difficult to contain my excitement when Everton's boss Billy Bingham confirmed that he would be happy to let me return to Scotland for the right price. I had not intended to seek a transfer, though it was clear that the new manager did not see me as part of his long-term plans. I would have toughed it out and forced him into a rethink because I was doing so well for Everton reserves or alternatively demonstrated my worth to other potential employers, but my wife's health had been poor since the birth of our son Ross, so I had to consider her wish to relocate closer to her nearest and dearest.

A rapid move back to Aberdeen, where we had always been happy, seemed to be the perfect solution and Billy promised to keep me informed while the clubs negotiated, but Hibernian boss Eddie Turnbull rather complicated the issue by calling me at home to ask if I would be willing to transfer to Easter Road instead. I repeat that Eddie was the best manager I played for and the opportunity to team up with him again was very tempting, but my heart was set on the Dons again, so I thanked him for his interest and took the cowardly option by saying that I would leave it up to Everton to decide where I moved. I was convinced that would be Pittodrie, so I was perturbed when Billy finally came back to me about a fortnight later to say that Hibs had topped Aberdeen's offer.

I discovered later that Everton had played one club against the other quite blatantly, which is understandable given that they had forked out a record £180,000 to sign me. The Dons had offered £90,000, Hibs had responded with £100,000, and this was followed by another Aberdeen bid of £110,000.

The war to clinch my services had raged on without my knowledge, but I was informed that Hibs had come up with an offer of £120,000, which Everton had agreed to accept. 'But I would rather go to Aberdeen,' I pleaded. To be fair to Billy, he agreed to discuss my departure with the Everton directors once more, but he returned about 15 minutes later to say: 'I'm sorry Joe, but if you want to back to Scotland I'm afraid you will have to go to Hibs.' A move to Hibs would certainly please Fiona, and by then Aberdeen had released a statement claiming that they had dropped their interest in me because they were unhappy that Everton had dragged them into an auction. I was despondent that my plan to move back to Pittodrie had been thwarted, but then I would be working for Eddie again and joining a side that were brimming with players of quality, including Pat Stanton, Erich Schaedler, Alan Gordon, Jimmy O'Rourke, Alex Cropley and Tony Higgins.

I agreed to travel to Carlisle to speak to Eddie and Hibs' owner and chairman, the millionaire businessman Tom Hart. During the journey to the north-west of England I was in a quandary over what to do for the best, for Aberdeen were my first choice. I resolved to ask Hibs for outrageous terms in the hope that they would drop their interest: 'I want the same wages and bonuses I'm on at Everton plus a £15,000 tax-free signing-on fee,' I demanded of Hart in the knowledge that this was well above what clubs such as Hibs were paying. I also insisted on the right to reside in the west, nearer to Glasgow than Edinburgh, which would suit my wife. 'Agreed,' Hart responded without so much as a blink of the eye, and it immediately crossed my mind that maybe I should have asked for more! Hart and Eddie presented detailed explanations of their determination to make Hibs the No. 1 side in Scotland. They had ended the 20-year trophy drought at Easter Road by beating Celtic in the League Cup final and had emerged as main challengers to the Glasgow side for the 1973-74 league title. We spoke for about an hour and I agreed to sign for Hibernian, settling terms that I could never have wrung from the Dons' chairman Dick Donald.

On returning to our house in Southport I was most upset when Fiona informed me that Aberdeen had called and urged me not to sign with Hibs just yet. They had apparently changed their minds and planned to make a final bid to persuade Everton to part with me, but mobile telephones had yet to come and she had no way of relaying the message to me in Carlisle.

I had signed for Hibs which left me in two minds: happy because I was about to rejoin Eddie, sad because I might well have returned to Aberdeen after all. The Dons directors were subjected to criticism from fans and the media for failing to gain my signature, but I learned that they did their best in difficult circumstances. They took the unusual step of releasing a statement the morning after my transfer to Hibernian:

> We have been negotiating with Everton for the past two months for the transfer of Joe Harper on the basis of a cash plus possible player exchange deal. This was then changed, at Everton's request, to a direct cash offer.
>
> We have made three cash offers, increasing each time, and our final bid last night was over £100,000. The club then found themselves in a direct auction with Hibs for the player, and it was decided to withdraw.'

I felt suitably deflated when I read that, but the deal had been done and in reality the prospect of playing for the Easter Road club was exciting, because they were a force to be reckoned with. Pat Stanton, the skipper who could perform in midfield or defence, is legendary because he was one of the most gifted players of his generation. Pat was backed up by John Blackley, a wonderful centre-back who should have gained more than seven Scotland caps, but was also clearly a victim of the bias against the less-fashionable clubs that I described earlier. I became particularly close to full-back Erich Schaedler, one of the toughest competitors Scottish football ever saw. He took no prisoners and I shudder at some of the tackles he put in. It was sad that Erich took his own life a few years later by turning a shotgun on himself, a horrific end for a man I recall as a gentleman and friend.

Hibs were particularly blessed with players who could create and score goals. Alex Edwards, who had made his debut for Dunfermline in a European tie against Valencia of Spain at the age of just 16, provided most of the ammunition from the right wing. Alex Cropley was an outstanding midfielder despite suffering three serious leg breaks in his career. Striker Alan Gordon had persuaded Hibs fans to overlook his spell at arch-rivals Hearts earlier in his career and was a firm favourite when I arrived. Also playing up front was Jimmy O'Rourke, a darling among Hibs followers after an outstanding display when they shattered Hearts in a 7-0 triumph at Tynecastle on New Year's Day 1973. They had become known as Turnbull's Tornadoes and I was delighted to join an exceptional squad.

As fate would have it, Hibs' first fixture after my transfer was scheduled at home versus Aberdeen in the league. It was weird sitting in the stand and being cheered by both sets of supporters; many Aberdeen fans I spoke to that day blamed the board's penny-pinching attitude for the fact that I had not returned to the north-east. Hibs won 3-1 and it was also weird trying to smile when the team that I preferred were on the receiving end.

I soon got down to work and anticipated a bright future with Hibs, but optimism turned to despair when over the next few months the club sold Brownlie, Cropley, Gordon and O'Rourke. Chairman Hart admitted that the business was required to claw back the fee the club had paid to me, so it was hardly surprising that I was seen as public enemy No. 1 by some supporters. One group who were particularly nasty towards me based themselves just under the old Main Stand at Easter Road. It did not matter what I did, they would boo and jeer and shout abuse: so much so that I came to hate them with a vengeance. I did my best to ignore the derision and was reasonably happy that I had at least helped Hibs to finish as championship runners-up to Celtic, who had achieved nine titles in a row. It was galling, though, that Hart had promised me a part within a side that would be the best in Scotland, which clearly would not come to fruition. Not to say that Hibernian had become a weak side, just that they would not be strong enough in all departments to lift the prize that I coveted most, the league title.

At the same time the majority of the Hibs support had decided that they would never take to Joe Harper, which was evident when we faced Dutch side Nijmegen in a friendly at Easter Road in August 1974. We won 5-0 and I scored all five and believed that achievement would finally help me to win over the fans. I was booed off the pitch, and the reaction was so vicious that Eddie Turnbull approached me to observe: 'You have to get away, don't you Joe?' I confirmed that I would be happy to move on, though I knew there was little chance of that happening in the near future because of the significant fee that Hibs had paid for me. I also had a professional duty to give the club a return on their investment, so I resolved to continue to try to score goals whether the fans liked me or not.

The opening league game of the 1974-75 season proved to be an odd experience because it was my first trip back to Pittodrie sporting the colours of another club. I'm pleased that I was at the top of my game and Aberdeen's defensive duo of Willie Miller and Willie Young were given a torrid time. The Dons were still winning 2-1 with four minutes to go, however, when we were awarded free-kick 25 yards from their goal. I informed my old pal Bobby Clark exactly where I intended to blast the ball past him into the goals, and he replied: 'Give it your best shot, wee man.' I did just that, and the ball rocketed past Bobby into the top corner to make it 2-2. It's the only goal of my career that I did not celebrate, and Hibs were not finished. On the stroke of full-time I fired in the ball and it hit Willie Young and dropped perfectly into the path of Alex Cropley, who claimed goal No. 3. The rest of the Hibs lads were delighted, but again I could not find it in me to celebrate. Aberdeen Football Club meant too much.

Personal highlights came in the UEFA Cup and Scottish League Cup. It was great to be back in Europe, drawn against Norwegian club Rosenborg, who are known nowadays as regulars in the Champions League. They were unfamiliar in 1975, but were anticipating making the next round despite losing 3-2 in Norway in the first leg. The return proved memorable for Hibs fans for their team beat Rosenborg 9-1, and I was delighted to get two goals. It remains Hibs' biggest victory in Europe and showed that we were still a pretty formidable force.

In the next round we were paired up with Juventus of Italy, who had beaten the Dons in the competition in 1972. Our hopes of doing well and enjoying a good season overall were not helped by the fixtures sequence, for we would be chasing Celtic in the league, facing Juventus the following Wednesday, then preparing to meet Celtic again in the League Cup final a few days before the return with the Italians. (Fixture problems encountered by Rangers in 2008 were not a new phenomenon). Hopes of making a positive start were dashed when Celtic hammered us 5-0 in the league in Glasgow, Dixie Deans claiming a hat-trick. We restored some pride against Juventus at Easter Road despite the presence of world-class performers such as Dino Zoff, Claudio Gentile and Roberto Bettega. We should have been awarded a penalty when my old chum Francesco Morini, who had inflicted private damage at the end of our match at Pittodrie, body-checked me inside the penalty-area. The referee, much to our fury, awarded an indirect free-kick for obstruction, and the Italians added to our ire by taking the lead through Gentile. We battled back to 2-1 thanks to goals from Pat Stanton and Alex Cropley. The Hibs fans were ecstatic, but Juventus showed their class by hitting us with a further three goals to win 4-2. They hammered us 4-0 in Italy, and 8-2 amounted to the biggest aggregate losing score Hibs have suffered in Europe.

I was heading towards another record as the first, and so far only, footballer to score a hat-trick in a major cup final in Scotland and still finish on the losing side. I have been asked many times if I was gutted after the 1975 League Cup final because I landed my first Hampden treble but no winners' medal, as Dixie Deans matched my feat to help Celtic to a 6-3 victory. The reply is always no, because I did my best on the day. My Hibs team-mates to a man also did their best to try to win the cup for what would have been the second time in three years for some. We just had the misfortune to face a Celtic side who were operating at their peak. Dixie did his bit close to goal, but wee Jimmy Johnstone was the star of that final. It was an honour to be on the pitch to witness a master winger at work as he tormented Hibs' defence from start to finish. He fired Celtic ahead after six minutes and Dixie made it 2-0 before I scored the first of my treble in advance of half-time. Paul Wilson restored his team's two-goal advantage, and I made it 3-2 on the hour, but Dixie then killed us off with two more inside a couple of minutes. My third and Celtic's sixth, scored by my former Aberdeen team-mate Steve Murray, proved academic and the better team lifted the trophy.

It was still an epic encounter that was helped greatly by the Scottish League altering the offside rule in the competition for that season. Players could be offside only within 18 yards from goal and a line was extended across the pitch to mark out the danger zones. It meant that strikers such as Dixie and I could poach well up the pitch, and the total of nine goals suggests the idea worked. This is probably the reason that the Scottish League returned to the old offside rule the following season.

Dixie, whose official name is John, and I have been great friends for many years, and he played for Neilston Juniors in the friendly match that provided my debut for Morton. I can reveal that Dixie and I had a personal wager based on the outcome of the 1975 final: whoever was on the winning side was obliged to pay for a slap-up meal that evening for both couples. Far from hiding away in the wake of defeat, Fiona and I made sure that Dixie contributed the bulk of his win bonus towards good food and expensive champagne. I have always admired Dixie whose Celtic goal tally of 132 in 184 appearances is incredible. He takes delight in reminding me that the hat-trick he nailed in 1975 made him the only player to score trebles in two major cup finals; his other hat-trick came in Celtic's 1972 Scottish Cup win over Hibs.

Dixie was still more popular with some of the Hibs fans than I was, and the sale of Alex Cropley for £150,000 to Arsenal in December led to more anger being directed towards me because he had been a Hibs hero for seven years. I was becoming increasingly unhappy, though I still sought to do my best in every game. The relationship with the chairman deteriorated when we reported for pre-season training in the summer of 1975 and I was sporting a full beard that I had grown during the holidays. I had become hairy for a laugh more than anything and planned to shave it off, but I changed my mind when Hart spotted the beard and in front of several witnesses and in a condescending manner ordered me to remove it. When I refused to do so, Hart said: 'Listen son, I own you because I paid for you to come to Hibs out of my own money. If I tell you to do something, you will just do it.' He was clearly trying to put me down in front of his pals, but I would have none of it. The row escalated and I made clear to the chairman that Hibs owned me and that as long as I was playing well and scoring goals, whether I had a beard or not had nothing to do with him. I also pointed out that Arthur Duncan and Erich Schaedler sported moustaches, but Hart went so far as banning me from taking part in the official photo-call which marked the start of every season. Eddie Turnbull was absent recovering from an operation, so a Hibs coach Wilson Humphries informed me that Hart had issued the ultimatum. Silly stuff, but I was 27-years-old and I was unaware of a club rule which ruled out facial hair. Some colleagues backed my stance to remain unshaven and declined to be photographed, which turned the event into a farce.

Hart was not finished. Hibs were due in Ireland for a pre-season tour, and he told me that if I did not remove the beard I would be left behind to train with the reserve and youth players. Now I certainly did not wish to miss the trip, which would have meant letting down Eddie who was preparing for the new season soon after surgery. I resolved to take things to the wire by turning up at the airport with beard still in place; I even fingered it and smiled when Hart walked past, glaring at me. Then I nipped into the toilet and shaved it off. Hart was livid when I revealed my new self with a cheery 'Morning chairman', and joined the lads queuing for the aircraft. I gathered from his look that my days at Easter Road were numbered.

I enjoyed another highlight of my career while still with

Hibernian in the early months of 1975-76, when we were drawn against Liverpool in the UEFA Cup. Scoring in the first leg when I struck Arthur Duncan's cross-pass beyond Ray Clemence was a great thrill for an Evertonian. We ran Liverpool ragged that night, and we would have travelled to Anfield with a healthier advantage but for John Brownlie's late penalty attempt being saved by Clemence. Eddie, as positive as ever, told us to go for a second goal in Liverpool, which let in John Toshack to make the aggregate 1-1, but the goal we wanted came via Alex Edwards, so Liverpool needed two to move forward. Toshack was the provider in completing a hat-trick of headers, but we were proud to have competed well against the team that went on to grasp the UEFA Cup that season. I also enjoyed the pleasure of scoring a screamer of a winner as we beat Hearts 1-0 in the Edinburgh derby, but Hibs fans still did not treat me as a favourite – especially not the hate brigade beneath the Main Stand who had targeted me. I was also forced to contend with the aftermath of the Copenhagen Affair, which I deal with in the next chapter, and this period developed into the most depressing of my career. Optimism would return only if I achieved a fresh start well away from that horrible batch of Hibs fans and inspired by supporters who had always delivered the backing on which I thrived, at Aberdeen Football Club.

An interview with the *Evening Express* in December 1975 carried out by Andy Melvin, who progressed to a major role at Sky Sports, hastened my departure from Edinburgh. Andy asked me if I was enjoying my time at Easter Road and I replied frankly: 'No, I have no peace of mind, and I'm sure the chairman doesn't like me. I will give everything while I'm still a Hibs player, but I would love to play for the Dons again.' That did not go down too well in the capital and I was dropped to the bench for Hibs' next game against Motherwell, then ordered to travel with the reserves the following week to face Celtic. I remained on the fringes of the first team as we moved into 1976, but it was evident that I would be moving sooner rather than later. My prayers were answered at the start of April when Hibs informed me that Aberdeen manager Ally MacLeod had asked if I would be willing to drive to Arbroath to speak to him.

15

THE COPENHAGEN FIVE

*'They have just announced you have been banned
for life from playing for Scotland'*

I contemplated walking away from professional football in 1975
because of the way I was treated in the wake of the Copenhagen
Affair. This book offers the first opportunity to set out details of
my side of the story because the Scottish Football Association
did not afford me that courtesy. The affair culminated with
Leeds United captain Billy Bremner, Celtic's Pat McCluskey, my
former Aberdeen team-mates Willie Young and Arthur Graham
and me being banned for life from playing for Scotland. We were
branded the Copenhagen Five and dealt with in this severe
fashion by the governing body for our alleged parts in an
incident at a nightclub in the Danish capital during the early
hours of Thursday, 4 September 1975.

I was with Hibs and had celebrated being recalled to Scotland
colours after a three-year absence by scoring the only goal
against Denmark in a European Championships qualifier. I
was delighted when manager Willie Ormond told us after the
game that we could let our hair down as a reward for recording a
crucial victory. Contrary to the vast collection of newspaper
reports that appeared later, Willie did not impose a 1 a.m.

curfew on any of us, but advised: 'Just make sure you are all back here by 10 a.m. for breakfast, because we head off for the airport an hour later.' We had the green light to enjoy ourselves instead of being confined to the team hotel, which was often normal practice. We ordered a fleet of taxis and fate bestowed that Billy, Pat, Willie, Arthur and I were grouped together in one of the cabs. The driver was asked to take us to wherever the other taxis had gone, but instead drove directly to a nightclub, assuring us we would be admitted because he knew the owner. It was well after midnight because kick-off had been timed for 8 p.m. and we had returned to the hotel to change; we hardly had a chance to embark on the 'boozy binge' that some reporters claimed had occurred.

We were desperate for a beer though, so we agreed to visit the nightclub and were disappointed to discover that it was practically empty. Billy, Pat and Willie made their way towards the bar, but Arthur and I were distracted when a Scotsman, who was sitting at a table in the far corner with another man, beckoned us to join him. It transpired that he was a businessman who had attended the match and the other individual was the owner of the club, who had moved to Denmark from Ireland. The owner was eager to hear my tale of how I had scored the winning goal for Scotland and ordered a bottle of expensive champagne, which Arthur and I enjoyed. Our chat was interrupted by a disturbance at the bar, where Billy, Pat and Willie were sipping beers. Willie, probably out of boredom because the place was so dead, had been gently tapping what I recall was a pen against one of the fancy designer light bulbs that were illuminating the bar. He must have hit it too hard because it broke. Willie offered to pay for the damage and was flabbergasted when the barman demanded the Danish equivalent of £800.

'I only want to pay for the bulb, I don't want to buy the place,' Willie exclaimed. The barman insisted and that sparked a reaction from Billy, who was a fiery character, and I was worried that something bad was about to kick off as Arthur and I moved to attempt to calm the situation.

Before we could do anything, eight policemen kitted out in riot gear came rushing in and pounced on Billy, Pat and Willie. Arthur and I had not been involved in any way, so they ignored us. I spotted a guy with braid on his hat and assumed that he was a senior officer. He spoke perfect English and reacted positively to my plea that we did not want any trouble because we were part of the Scotland team that had played against Denmark the previous night. I added: 'I will make sure the damage is paid for, and that everyone goes straight back to the team hotel.' The officer agreed to this plan of action, so we made to follow the other policemen who were escorting Billy, Pat and Willie out of the nightclub via the spiral staircase that led to the street. I could see one of them was being particularly rough with Pat and had rammed one of his arms up his back. Pat got annoyed and shoved back at the officer; Billy and Willie moved in to help. Now I don't know if any punches were thrown, but by the time Arthur and I had made it out to the street with the senior officer, Billy, Pat and Willie were lying handcuffed over police-car bonnets. The senior man quickly calmed things down and ordered the three lads to be released. He turned to me and said: 'Go now, but never come back into the centre of Copenhagen.'

We were not charged, so I was praying that would be the last we would hear of the incident. The madness of the night was not over, though. When we got back to the hotel, Billy, who was always up for a bit of a prank, spotted the door to one of the single rooms had been left open. Pat and I did our best to make him see reason, but our skipper was having none of it and began to turn the bed and furniture upside down and to throw the guest's clothes all over the place. Unfortunately the occupant was SFA committee member Jock McDonald, a giant of a man who was chairman of Highland League side Inverness Thistle. He later held the same post when the club merged with Inverness Caledonian to gain entry to the Scottish League, and he was now standing at the door watching Billy trying to wreck his room. Billy attempted to make a joke of it, but Jock was not amused and promptly employed a right hook to lay out the Scotland captain cold. I am not exaggerating, for Jock did knock Billy flat, then ordered Pat and me to pick him up and to head for bed. I was worried about the repercussions because Jock was a leading light with the SFA, but he soon calmed down and joined us later in another room for a drink and chat about football. When we gathered to prepare for the trip home no one mentioned the nightclub incident, and Jock, to his credit, had not complained about Billy's actions.

I believed that nothing more would come of it, and returned to duty with Hibs, eager to prove that scoring for Scotland would have a positive spin-off. Unfortunately we lost 1-0 away to Dundee United in the league the following Saturday and I was back at my house in Glasgow feeling down when I received a telephone call from my journalist pal in Aberdeen, Ian Broadley. Ian and I played golf on Sundays if he was in my part of the country, and I was just about to tell him that I was not in the mood to swing a club when he asked: 'Have you any comment to make about the ban, Joe?'

I asked what ban and he replied: 'The one from the SFA. They have just announced you have been banned for life from playing for Scotland.'

I was stunned into silence, then a sense of anger pulsed through my body.

Ian explained that the SFA had decided to hold a meeting on the Saturday afternoon after they had been informed about a serious incident involving some Scotland players in the nightclub

in Copenhagen. A statement released by the association confirmed that we had been banned for that and another incident
when some of us had 'been discovered in the bedroom of one of
the SFA's travelling party'. None of us was informed that a
meeting had been arranged, so we were not given the chance to
explain our side of the story

It should be noted that the SFA had been criticised for failing
to take action against Celtic's Jimmy Johnstone for his part in a
well-publicised prank when the Scotland squad had been resident at Largs the year before. Willie Ormond, as he did in
Copenhagen, allowed the players to head off for a few beers after
they had beaten Wales 2-0 at Hampden. After leaving the pub
Jimmy had spotted a rowing boat tied up in the harbour and
decided to borrow it. He realised too late that the boat had no
oars, and he was eventually rescued by the coastguard before he
drifted into the open sea. Typically, Jimmy laughed off the
occurrence by claiming that he could not understand what all
the fuss was about: he had decided to do a bit of fishing. No
harm was done and the wee winger proved that by playing a
starring role when Scotland beat England 2-0 at Hampden the
following Saturday.

Whispers arose that the SFA planned to come down hard on
anyone who stepped out of line in the future, and the Copenhagen incident provided the perfect opportunity. News of the
ban was plastered all over the Sunday papers, and I was
particularly worried about how my Dad would react. On
the previous Thursday his workmates at the shipyard had
formed a guard of honour for the father of the player who
had scored the winner for Scotland. Now he would have to
endure embarrassing questions about what had led to me being
banned for life.

Most press reports claimed that the ban had been imposed
because all five of us had become involved in a drunken brawl

and had caused damage at the nightclub. That was infuriating because I knew that Arthur and I were innocent of any wrongdoing, and I considered the SFA action to be extremely harsh considering that Danish police had merely sent us on our way. The incident in Jock McDonald's room, while childish, was hardly serious enough to merit such a hefty punishment either, particularly when I knew that Arthur and Willie were not present. But the SFA's failure to invite us to the hearing to defend ourselves angered me most of all. Their offices were closed on Sunday, so I was forced to wait until Monday morning to make phone contact with Ernie Walker, who was assistant secretary of the SFA but already a powerful figure behind the scenes. I asked Ernie if I could meet with the SFA that day, but he refused:

JOE HARPER: '*You can't just ban me without allowing me the right to argue my case.*'
ERNIE WALKER: '*Yes we can. We make the rules, so we can do anything we like.*'

Ernie hung up. I was near bursting with rage and contacted lawyer Margaret Dale, a friend of the family. When I explained the situation she agreed that the SFA were out of order, and they were eventually persuaded to meet her. But that did not go too well either. She maintained that my only crime had been to be in the wrong place at the wrong time:

ERNIE WALKER: '*Tough luck on Joe. We won't change our mind, and if he decides to make a fuss about any of this, you can tell him I will personally guarantee he will never play for Scotland again.*'

When Margaret relayed that quote I was baffled by Ernie's threat, because I had been banned for life already. I was devastated, especially when Scottish Television broadcast an item that included their news crew visiting the nightclub. They went on a Friday night and it was heaving, but Fiona believed me when I insisted that it had been practically empty during the early hours of the Thursday.

My next step was to try to convince Billy, Pat and Willie at least to back up the claims from Arthur and me that we were totally innocent. I wrote to Leeds United asking if I could meet Billy. I sent a letter to Celtic asking the same of Pat, and another to Spurs who had signed Willie from Aberdeen. I felt it would be best to meet all three face to face, but Leeds and Celtic refused and Tottenham did not have the courtesy to reply. Arthur and I decided to lodge appeals anyway, and we learned that Willie had also decided to do that. Billy and Pat chose to accept the bans, which was particularly sad for the former who was a magnificent captain and leader of the Scotland over many years and was one cap short of the record of 54 set by Denis Law. A Danish journalist who had been present at the club presented a letter detailing what had happened and making clear that Arthur and I had done nothing wrong. The SFA refused to accept the document, and our appeals heard on 16 October 1975 were rejected. I use the term *heard* loosely. We had to write letters to the SFA putting forward our versions of what had transpired in Copenhagen, but we were not offered the opportunity of speaking to them directly. That was the final straw for me, a denial of natural justice, and I was so disgusted by the episode that I decided to quit football.

My father-in-law ran a successful engineering company in Renfrewshire, and I told Fiona that I would to ask for a job. I also sounded out my best pal Ally Kennedy, an Aberdeen businessman, but he and my wife advised me not to be rash, arguing that if I walked away from football I would regret it for the rest of my life. Ally also pointed out, sagely, that my retirement might please some people at the SFA because it would mean my giving up the fight to clear my name.

That was enough to make me change my mind, and I also let it be known within football circles that I intended to take the SFA to court. The situation changed dramatically when I received a telephone call at home late at night a couple of weeks later. It was a member of the Kelly family, who were heavily involved with Celtic and the SFA at the time. To my eternal frustration I cannot recall which of the Kellys made the call, but I remember the gist of the conversation all right. I was assured that the SFA ban would remain and that the situation would only get worse for me if I chose to take matters further:

MIDNIGHT CALLER: *'We know you and Arthur Graham did nothing wrong, but if you decide to take things to court you will never play for Scotland again. Do nothing, and I promise you the ban on you both will be lifted within a year.'*

The caller ended by reminding me that no record of our conversation would exist, so he would deny that it had happened if it was made public. I was left in a difficult position: I could go to the expense and effort of taking the SFA to court, with no real evidence that I could win. They certainly had far more resources than I had at my disposal. The other option was to bite my tongue and be content that in a year's time the SFA would be making a statement that would clear Arthur and me, with the bonus that we would be eligible to play for our country again. I chose this option, though I must emphasise that I believed that pressure would be exerted on future Scotland managers to pick anyone but Arthur Graham or Joe Harper.

As the Midnight Caller had indicated, the bans *were* lifted a little over 12 months later, the SFA maintaining in their wisdom that they felt the punishments had served their purpose. Much to my amazement I was selected for Scotland again, but I cannot claim that the international honour brought any favours with it. My fourth Scotland cap, which would prove to be my last, came during that ill-fated trip to the 1978 World Cup finals in Argentina.

16

CRAZY DAYS WITH ALLY

*'The manager was at his eccentric best
for the final at Hampden'*

My football career after Copenhagen did not regain proper
momentum until I had secured a return to Aberdeen. When
Eddie Turnbull told me that I had permission to meet Ally
MacLeod, I knew that I was heading home from Hibs. At the
hotel in Arbroath, which is south of Aberdeen, he was sitting at a
table with a pot of tea and two cups. I accepted the offer of a cup
and sat down beside the man who had been appointed as Jimmy
Bonthrone's successor at Pittodrie that season. 'I want you to
sign for Aberdeen again,' said Ally getting right to the point.
'Okay,' I replied and shook his hand, which seemed to surprise
him. All over in less than 10 seconds without even discussing
terms, though I told Ally: 'Just pay me the same basic I'm on at
Hibs. I will trust you to sort out the bonuses and anything else.'

We spoke for a few minutes, but the next step in my career had
been sorted out. I had made my mind up the second that Eddie
had informed me of the potential move, though a spanner might
have been thrust into works. What many Dons fans do not know
is that originally Aberdeen were seeking to swap me for Davie
Robb, but he did not want a job at Easter Road. The clubs kept

talking and settled on a fee of £50,000, which made a total of £90,000 that the Dons had paid for me over two deals. Place that beside the £180,000 that they had earned when I signed for Everton and the club record of 205 goals that I recorded, and I reckon their return was worthwhile. And you can add the fact that Davie Robb would prove to be a Hampden goal hero before the year was out.

Only after I had signed did it dawn on me that the deal had been completed after the March 31 registration deadline, so I would be unable to play another first-team game in the current season. That was of no concern for I was returning to my spiritual home and was sure that Dons fans would be won over when I got going during the following season. Reaction from the Red Army was evident more immediately, and caused me astonishment. I was permitted to appear in reserve matches for Aberdeen and attendances for those rocketed. I was mobbed when I scored in the last minute against St Johnstone, and more than 5,000 turned up to watch me hit the net four times in a 5-0 success over Celtic.

The reaction helped to take my mind off the fact that the Dons were in imminent danger of being relegated for the first time, which was an amazing predicament considering the advanced position that they had occupied on my departure for Everton in 1972. Ally had at least raised confidence, but survival depended on beating Hibs at Pittodrie on the final day of the season. I did my bit in the dressing-room to gee up the troops. I did not wish to be cast into a lower division, and certainly not by the club I had left recently. I sat nervously in the Main Stand praying for the right result, and victory by 3-0 sent Dundee down on goal difference.

I was confident that close calls would be avoided in future, and not just because I was aiming to land loads of goals. The squad had changed considerably in the four years that I had been away, but Davie Robb, Drew Jarvie and Bobby Clark remained to offer much-needed experience. Willie Miller was captain and sweeper, which made a sweeping change from the days when he had operated as a young striker in the reserves and his allotted tasks included polishing my boots. Willie was the finest penalty-box defender of his generation, a professional of great determination, and I cannot recall him losing a one-on-one tussle with a striker. He was not the type of individual who could tolerate Aberdeen being dispatched to the wrong end of the league again. Ally also brought in Stuart Kennedy from Falkirk and Clyde's Dom Sullivan, so we were in good shape for 1976-77.

Unfortunately Willie Miller had been banned for the first three games of the season which were League Cup ties, and I was gratified when Ally appointed me captain in his absence. I scored in each as we beat Kilmarnock 2-0 at Pittodrie, St Mirren 3-2 away and finished with a 1-0 home victory over Ayr United. I still take great delight in the assertion that, as far as I know, I am the only undefeated captain in Aberdeen's history, and the sequence provided the perfect start to what became a thrilling campaign under Ally's management. He was certainly different as a football gaffer, but he was not given appropriate credit for transforming the Dons' fortunes in the 1970s. His enthusiasm for the game was infectious and his influence had the city of Aberdeen buzzing with excitement. Ally did not claim to be the greatest coach, but he did possess the vital knack of motivating all who worked with him and we would have done anything for the man because we loved him.

Ally MacLeod hauled Aberdeen from the brink of relegation to clinching the Scottish League Cup within a few months. He also signed players who helped immediate successors Billy McNeill and Alex Ferguson to take the club to another level, and rightly deserves a place of honour in the Pittodrie archives. Some of Ally's training methods were remarkable and included arranging training on the beach when the tide was in, but then he was too proud to admit that he could not work out the timing of the ebb and flow of the waves. He justified his methods by claiming that running in the sea was ideal for strengthening the legs and we attempted to play football with salt water up to our knees – a player would be ordered to swim for the ball if he sent it splashing into the deep.

Now any brave soul who has ventured to Aberdeen beach will confirm that the water is extremely cold even at the height of summer, but Ally took us there only when snow and ice ruled out the use of grass training areas. We played head tennis in the Pittodrie car park when it was covered with deep snow, and we also had to contend with Ally's end-of-session bounce games, which are the stuff of legend. The manager always took part and tended to keep them going until his team had won. He cheated incessantly and antagonised Bobby Clark, who took seriously every game in which he played. If Ally's team were losing he would throw in a rule, usually when he was about to score, that the next goal would count five, and at the final whistle he celebrated as if he had won a cup final. Bobby marked off the proper score in the sand beside his goal, and tended to storm off the training pitch in protest over the manager's ploys to ensure that his team emerged victorious. That would bring on that famous broad grin, and Ally revealed to me later that he merely was ensuring that Bobby's hunger to win stayed strong. Crazy days, but we were delighted to go along with Ally because Pittodrie was again a happy place at which to work.

Ally also demonstrated distinctive methods of punishing players who stepped out of line, as centre-half Willie Garner was dismayed to find out. His problems stemmed from accepting a lift home to Glasgow from the manager, who was heading for Ayr after a festive-season game at Pittodrie. Willie was told to go easy on the celebrations, but come Monday morning he arrived late at the pick-up point for the return trip north, and he was a bit worse for wear. Sick, you might say, and the car trip had to be interrupted while Willie attempted to recover. Well, Ally was not chuffed and put Willie through the mill at training, but he seemed to have forgiven his unprofessional conduct until our centre-half blew it in the usual match that ended our stint. I was in a team with Ally and Willie, and we were losing by 15-12 in the dying seconds when I found myself through on the goal-keeper with the manager roaring that the next goal was 'worth three'. I duly scored to make it 15-15 according to Ally's reckoning, and we eventually moved into a dramatic, sudden-death penalty shoot-out. The manager was about to step up to take the crucial kick when Willie grabbed the ball from him with the plea: 'Let me take it gaffer. I've never missed a penalty.' Ally responded with: 'After all you've put me through today you better score, or I will have you in for extra training tonight.' Willie's vital shot was saved.

Pittodrie was in complete darkness that night, dressing-room included, for Ally had no idea how to switch on the power, and Willie was ordered to start lapping the pitch in the gloom. He thought it would be safe to slow down a little when he got to the point furthest away from the tunnel where Ally had been standing. He almost died of fright when the manager jumped up from behind the terracing wall and ordered him to stop slacking; Ally had sneaked across the pitch in the darkness to check on the penal regime. He repeated the process a few more times, and Willie became more alarmed about where Ally would pop up next than about the extra work he was enduring! A sprinkling of snow had landed on Pittodrie that mid-winter night, and next day we were amused to trace the footprints left as evidence by the boss, who had probably covered more distance than the man he was disciplining.

Ally also promoted some strange ideas when it came to trying to win matches for real. For corner-kicks he came up with the follow-the-leader routine in which some players formed a pack at the edge of the penalty-area, then broke out at the last second to set positions from which they hoped to meet the cross. In the year 2000 praise was heaped on Aberdeen's Danish manager Ebbe Skovdahl for just such a manoeuvre, but Ally had beaten him to it years before. Older fans will remember how Ally arranged for the entire team to line up along the halfway line when we kicked off, the plan being to kick the ball down the wing as quickly as possible and for players to chase it like madmen. Ally claimed that it would unnerve opponents if they saw that Aberdeen were willing to have a go right from the start, and he also argued that attacking immediately would get Dons fans springing to their feet and enhance the match atmosphere. I must admit to bungling one of those passes forward, against Hearts as I recall, and it allowed our opponents to race forward unchallenged and to score after some 24 seconds. Ally almost strangled me afterwards, but he continued to orchestrate the cavalry charges.

My hopes of a dream return that season were shattered on the morning of 16 October 1976, when the family were hit by a tragedy that still hurts to the core. I was at home with my wife Fiona watching the television news, which included a report on a fatal road accident at Cumbernauld near Glasgow. I recall saying it was terrible before heading for bed early because the Dons were due to play Rangers at Pittodrie the next day. I was wakened by the phone just after 6 in the morning, and Fiona's father informed us that her sister Katie and family had been involved in the accident. Katie was badly injured, but her husband Sandy, 37, and children Jill, 9, Andrew, 8, and Anne, 4, were killed. We were devastated, and when I contacted Ally he told me to take as much time off as I needed. The press were informed that I would miss the game because of injury. It was an awful time, particularly for poor Katie, but I have always admired the strength that she showed in such adversity, and she later remarried. I was disgusted when a journalist from the far north of Scotland phoned me on the Sunday claiming that he had heard from a good source that I had been dropped from the Rangers game because I had been out drinking on Friday night. I dread to think what I would have done if I had been face to face with the journalist that day.

You can never forget a tragedy, but we got on with our lives as best we could. The family agreed that I should start by turning out for the Dons the following Monday in their League Cup quarter-final replay at Dens Park, Dundee. Ally assured me that he would understand if I wanted to leave it a little longer, but I chose to give it a go and helped to set up a goal for Jocky Scott. I was hardly in the mood to celebrate our 2-0 victory that booked a semi-final showdown with Rangers at Hampden. That proved to be one of the greatest games in Aberdeen's history, however, and I much appreciated my Pittodrie mates rallying behind me, which boosted my spirits by the time of the semi-final. We won 5-1 and our tally included a Drew Jarvie screamer of a volley from the edge of Rangers' penalty-area and a strike from me, but Jocky Scott stole the show with a hat-trick, and I must admit that qualifying for a cup final in the month of that awful accident created a strange feeling within me. At the final whistle Ally danced with delight across the Hampden pitch, and he forecast: 'We will win the cup now.'

Some observers found that hard to believe for we would be facing Celtic, who were heading for another league and Scottish Cup double that season. The manager was at his eccentric best for the final at Hampden on 6 November 1976. We spent the night before at a hotel and were mystified when Ally ordered our bus to stop on the hard shoulder of the M8 as we made for the national stadium. He produced a massive walkie-talkie, a forerunner of the mobile phone, and yelled into it: 'Are they there yet?' We could not make out the crackling response, but Ally suddenly shouted at the driver: 'Go, go, go!' Our bus rejoined the motorway – bang in front of the Celtic coach which was forced to brake. We completed the journey to Hampden with Ally constantly peering through the back window and ordering our driver to proceed this way or that to ensure that our opponents' bus could not overtake. I could see via the back window that manager Jock Stein and other Celtic officials were livid, but when we arrived at the stadium Ally proclaimed from the front of our bus: 'Right lads, we've beaten them to Hampden, now let's beat them at Hampden.'

It was a year to the day since Ally had taken over an Aberdeen side who badly needed hauling up by their bootstraps, so we were desperate that our gaffer should be rewarded. I can reveal an omen that this would be so. Bobby Clark, Davie Robb and I were enjoying breakfast that morning when Bobby suddenly turned to Davie and said: 'I dreamt last night that you came off the bench and scored the winner today.' Now there are more beautiful figures to dream about than big Davie and the man in question was certainly not happy at the suggestion from our goalkeeper that he would be acting as a substitute, because he had expected to be on the park from the start of the final. A few hours on, much to his displeasure, Davie discovered that he would be occupying the bench. The starting XIs were:

Aberdeen: Bobby Clark, Stuart Kennedy, Bobby Williamson, Joe Smith, Willie Garner, Willie Miller, Dom Sullivan, Jocky Scott, Drew Jarvie, Joe Harper and Arthur Graham.

Celtic: Peter Latchford, Danny McGrain, Andy Lynch, Johannes Edvaldsson, Roddie MacDonald, Roy Aitken, John Doyle, Ronnie Glavin, Kenny Dalglish, Tommy Burns and Paul Wilson.

I would love to say that we were magnificent at Hampden, but that would be mere hyperbole. Celtic would have put us to the sword had it not been for outstanding displays by Bobby Clark, Willie Miller and the rest of our defenders. Kenny Dalglish threw himself to the ground after he was challenged by Drew Jarvie to win a penalty, and we were still fuming at what appeared to be a blatant dive when Kenny recovered to slot the spot-kick past Bobby. We equalised against the run of play when Arthur Graham's cross reached me at the back post. I faced a tight angle to the Celtic goal from which it would have been mighty hard to score, so I nodded the ball across for Drew Jarvie who completed the move with a forceful header. Celtic battered us from all angles with John Doyle, Paul Wilson and their substitute veteran Bobby Lennox all going close, but we held firm to take the action into extra-time. By then Davie Robb had emerged from dreamland to replace Drew Jarvie, and within minutes of the restart Arthur Graham showed his class by leaving the great Danny McGrain in his wake as he fashioned a fine run across the pitch from the left to right wing. Arthur fired the ball to my feet at the edge of the Celtic six-yard box and I had the goal at my mercy. I have always maintained that I spotted Davie out of the corner of my eye so laid the ball on to him, but it is time to confess to fluffing it. I wanted to burst the Celtic net, but my timing was awry and the ball rolled to Davie off my shin for him to bundle it over the line from a couple of yards. Not pretty, but it won the Scottish League Cup.

I remember aiming a telling look towards Bobby Clark when the final whistle was blown and we began to celebrate. It was quite spooky that he had predicted what would happen. Ally ran about hugging every player and was more excited than anyone. He did things differently, but he had proved that his methods of management worked, and clinching that cup so soon after the Dons had escaped relegation, only just, was a great achievement.

Hampden success delivered a lift in our fight to stay in the hunt for the league title, and I experienced the joy of scoring what many regard as my best goal when we met my previous club Hibs at Pittodrie. I waltzed past three visiting players then whacked a 25-yard shot into the net for a 1-0 victory. My delight intensified when television highlights confirmed that I had caught out the commentator as he described the action:

ARCHIE MACPHERSON: *'There's Joe Harper, we've certainly not seen much of Scotland's top scorer today . . . Oh, what a goal!'*
VERDICT OF ALLY MACLEOD: *'That was the best goal I've seen. It's a goal only Joe Harper could have scored.'*

Victory thrust us to the top of the division ahead of Dundee United on goal difference, but we could not sustain our challenge. We finished third behind the Old Firm, but it made for a marked improvement on where the Dons had ended up a year previously and I was proud to have ended the season as Scotland's top scorer with 28 goals in all competitions, two ahead of Celtic's Ronnie Glavin and Joe Craig. I was enjoying being back at my spiritual home and Ally was talking of making some big signings. He had also blooded Doug Rougvie and John McMaster, which meant that four of the future Gothenburg Greats – the others being Willie Miller and Stuart Kennedy – were in the side.

In the context of the Scottish Cup, I was angered by a newspaper's claims that arose after Dundee had recorded a shock 2-1

replay victory over Aberdeen at Pittodrie on Wednesday, 2 March 1977. We beat Celtic 2-0 in the league in another home match the following Saturday, but my pride was dented by a television advertisement for the Scottish *Sunday Mail*, which was broadcast in the evening as I viewed with my family. 'Dons players in cup betting sensation. Read all about it tomorrow,' the announcer declared before claiming that this was a story no Dons fan would want to miss. All those connected with Pittodrie were infuriated next day by a report which claimed an Aberdeen fan had overheard four players, including myself and goalkeeper Bobby Clark, using a public phone box immediately outside Pittodrie to place a big bet on Dundee to win the fourth-round replay. It was complete nonsense, and I know for a fact that Bobby has never gambled on anything. We still had to undergo the indignity of being interviewed by police, though they informed us that they thought the story was complete fiction. We were all cleared of any wrongdoing, but the incident made me wary of dealing with certain newspapers and journalists for the rest of my career. It demonstrated why I did not bet on *any* game in which I played. I stuck to the inexact science of wagering on the horses.

The manager decided to celebrate our earlier Scottish League Cup success by taking us on an end-of-season trip to Yugoslavia. We were ordered to report for training at 8.30 a.m. on the first day and were taken aback when Ally ordered a round of beers and announced that he had agreed to take over as manager of Scotland. He thanked us all for what we had done for him and he was sure that our next manager would enjoy great success because we were special players. We were sad to see him go, but the lure of managing the national side was too strong to turn down. The pain of loss evaporated when we heard that Aberdeen had chosen Billy McNeill as the new manager. The former Celtic and Scotland skipper was an icon as the first man to captain a British club to success in the European Cup, and I held him in the highest respect. I have come to regard him as a close friend over the years; he was tough but fair as an opponent and a fine manager. Billy came as a contrast to Ally MacLeod for he was meticulous in preparation and an outstanding tactician, and his stature was such that he only had to walk into a room to command respect. It was a major disappointment that we failed to deliver a trophy for him because he proved in his one season with the Dons that he was an inspiration from the dug-out. Billy was never a shouter in the manner of Eddie Turnbull or Alex Ferguson who would succeed him at Pittodrie. He left that to assistant John Clark while he got his point across with quiet authority, and we were impressed by the way he altered tactics time and again to help to win games in which we had been struggling.

Billy began with a handicap because my good friend Arthur Graham, who had given the Dons sterling service since playing in the 1970 Scottish Cup final as a teenager, chose to move to Leeds United. Billy had a great eye for a footballer though. He signed Steve Archibald, who had played for him at Clyde, bringing on board a magnificent striker who would help the Dons to win the league in 1980 and then be sold to Tottenham Hotspur for £900,000. Not a bad piece of business overall. Billy also brought in one of the greatest players to wear an Aberdeen shirt in Gordon Strachan. A fair number of supporters criticised the decision to swap Jim Shirra for Gordon, who was with Dundee, but Billy assured us from day one that the wee man would become a star. Billy also handed an Aberdeen debut to a teenage defender named Alex McLeish and ensured that John McMaster was a permanent fixture in the first team.

We were a whisker away from landing a league and cup double for the first time in the club's history, and that after receiving heavy flak when Rangers beat us 6-1 in the League Cup. We embarked on a 23-match unbeaten run in the league to take the race to the last day. We had to overcome Hibs at Easter Road and to hope that Rangers would slip up at home to Motherwell. We drew 1-1 and Rangers won 2-0, so the Ibrox club would have taken the trophy anyway, but it was frustrating to be pipped by two points. We were determined to gain revenge when we faced Rangers in the Scottish Cup final at Hampden the following weekend. Billy presented an inspiring pre-match speech and it was quite obvious that he wished to steal a trophy away from the club that he had deflated many times as a player. He did all he could to send us on to the pitch in the right frame of mind, but we simply froze and performed like a bunch of rabbits caught in headlights. We let down Billy and our fans. Badly. Our performance was summed up by full-back Steve Ritchie pulling off a joke of a goal when his scooped shot soared sky-high before dropping behind Rangers' goalkeeper Peter McCloy to make the score 2-1.

We were an embarrassment to all and sundry at Hampden and I was furious that we had failed Billy, who was used to more successful outcomes. And yet he had performed remarkably well for his first season, and I'm sure that he would have led the Dons to unprecedented success during the 1980s had he stayed in charge. Unfortunately for Aberdeen the great Jock Stein had decided it was time to step down at Celtic, and Billy McNeill provided the obvious successor. For the second summer in a row we were left to wonder who would become our next manager. I was pleased that the directors went for Alex Ferguson, who had shown ambition and hunger when boss of St Mirren. I was eager to start work with the new gaffer, but the initial priority was a trip to South America with the Scotland party.

17

OFF TO ARGENTINA

*'Most followers of the game felt that Ally
had made the right choices'*

It infuriates me that Ally MacLeod carried the can for Scotland's
embarrassment and shame at the 1978 World Cup finals in
Argentina.

That tournament broke Ally's spirit and he was never the
same man in the aftermath, which is extremely sad, and added to
my feelings of guilt when I attended his funeral in 2004. The
national manager was accused of failing the Scottish nation, but
he was let down by the Scottish squad, including me, who failed
to deliver performances that his loyalty deserved in facing Peru
and Iran. He was also let down by the Scottish Football Association, who were responsible for arranging the trip and who
proved in the terms of the meaningful phrase that they could not
organise a piss-up in a brewery. Ally was also undermined by the
Scottish media who acted as best friends when it suited them, but
then attacked the man like vultures picking over carrion. The
much-heralded Tartan Army also let Ally down by turning on
him with a vengeance when his only significant fault was
offering them some hope.

I was sad for Aberdeen Football Club but delighted for Ally

when he quit in May 1977 to take over as Scotland boss. His infectious enthusiasm had proved a godsend for the Dons, though it was a shame in retrospect that he did not get the chance to build on whatever success he had enjoyed during his brief spell in the Granite City. I recall feeling proud for Ally that his efforts had been enough to warrant a tilt at the Scotland job which he saw as the professional pinnacle. Seventeen matches and a little over 500 days later he was forced to go into hiding because he was seen as public enemy No. 1 within our nation. I now have the opportunity to put the record straight and to explain why it was wrong for Ally to be made the scapegoat. I accept that I may be seen as biased because he had served as a popular gaffer at Aberdeen and was kind enough to offer me my fourth, and last, cap. So be it, but what follows is my version of Scotland's disastrous Argentinean adventure, and I hope that it will support my view that Ally MacLeod should be remembered as one of the greatest managers of the Scotland team.

My delight at being recalled to the fold was heightened because I had believed that though the life ban in the wake of the Copenhagen debacle had been lifted, the SFA's big-wigs would ensure by devious means that I did not kick a ball again in the national cause. Ally had obviously noted that I was scoring plenty of goals for Aberdeen – 28 in the only full season that I played under him – and I took a place on the bench when Scotland faced Wales at Anfield in October 1977 to contest the right to proceed to the World Cup finals in Argentina the following year.

The Welsh FA made a serious miscalculation by moving the game from a smaller stadium in the principality, say in Cardiff or Wrexham, to exploit the intense interest engendered among Scottish followers. Liverpool's home was packed to its 51,000 capacity, with Scots by far in the majority, and lions rampant and tartan were resplendent in all areas of the ground. The noise created by our fans was ear-splitting – I was in the midst of it – and without doubt the vocal force helped to drive us to victory that night. My old pal Alan Rough could be mocked for some performances in goal, but he made one of the finest saves that I witnessed in my professional career to keep Scotland's World Cup bandwagon on track. Striker John Toshack hit a tremendous shot which Alan somehow managed to direct over his crossbar, and the value of the heroic act was highlighted with 11 minutes to go when we were awarded a penalty, the referee ruling that Welsh defender David Jones had handled the ball as he tussled with Joe Jordan. That decision has been the subject of great debate over the years, and Welsh interests continue to insist that they were robbed because big Joe did the handling. They are right to feel cheated. I don't think that Joe has confessed on the record that he was indeed the guilty party, but he admitted it openly in the dressing-room after the game. I certainly believed that it was Joe's hand that had been raised when I watched the incident live. None of us cared because a place at the World Cup was at stake, and I darted off the bench to join the celebrations when Don Masson took full advantage of the penalty award. Victory was assured late on when my former Dons team-mate Martin Buchan sent in a magnificent cross from the right wing for Kenny Dalglish to head home and make it 2-0.

I was by no means certain to be heading down South America way at that juncture. I had been included in an initial group of 40, and Ally took the unusual step of cutting numbers to 21 while announcing that the final spot would be allocated to another striker. The media speculated that the candidates were Joe Harper, Aston Villa's Andy Gray and Coventry City's Ian Wallace, but we were kept on tenterhooks. Ally still had not revealed his choice when I attended the Player of the Year dinner at the Albany Hotel, Glasgow, at the end of season 1977-78. He was lined up as a guest speaker and as I was heading into the toilet he put a hand on my shoulder and said: 'Listen Joe, away and phone your mum and dad and tell them you are going to Argentina for your summer holidays.' I was stunned and only too happy to agree when Ally asked me to tell no one but my closest family because he had to arrange an official announcement. It made big news next day and Andy Gray, in particular, was most unhappy. He had scored 29 goals for Villa and been selected as England player of the year and young player of the year, a double that was unique until Manchester United's Cristiano Ronaldo achieved it in 2008. I could understand Ally's choice, for Andy was more of a target-man, and Scotland had Jordan and Rangers' Derek Johnstone as regulars in the squad. He was looking for back-up to Kenny Dalglish, and that role was more suited to Ian or me. I was just grateful to get the nod.

I cannot recall too much criticism when the 22-man squad were confirmed. Most followers of the game felt that Ally had made the right choices, though on reflection he was perhaps too loyal to some of the guys who had taken Scotland through the qualifying stages. One in that category was defender Gordon McQueen, who had picked up an injury and had no chance of being fit for the finals. Ally stuck by him as he did with Don Masson, who had done his bit and should have been moved aside to make way for Graeme Souness, the rising star among Scottish midfielders. That was Ally's biggest weakness: if he felt individuals had done well for him, he would bend over backwards to repay that loyalty. And he piled up the pressure on his shoulders by telling the press that he believed we could come back from Argentina with a medal.

Now Ally's stated view has been transformed and exaggerated in some accounts into boasts from the manager that we would go on to win the World Cup, which he did not actually say. 'In the past we have blown our chances with silly mistakes, like those against Zaire in 1974,' he reflected. 'This time, I promise we won't throw away the golden opportunity.' When pressed to say if he thought Scotland would win the tournament, Ally replied: 'Someone has to, so why not us? We will do our best, and I do think we are capable of getting some sort of medal if everything falls into place.' He was not alone in expressing optimism. Why not? Scotland could field some cracking players and had run mighty Brazil close in drawing 0-0 at the 1974 finals in West Germany. If the Scots had performed at the peaks of their potential and had remained resolutely united as a team, they *could* have claimed medals. That scenario did not come to fruition, and we ended up with tears for souvenirs plus spittle down our blue shirts from Scotland fans having a go at us. Sad, but true.

A divide between Anglo-Scots and home-based men was usually evident when Scotland squads gathered. It was not inevitably a big gap, but it was pretty bad when the squad met up at Dunblane Hydro Hotel to discuss bonuses that would be paid to players for participating in the finals, which would boost the SFA coffers considerably.

Most home Scots, including me, were not too concerned about the issue, and I would probably have been happy to pay for the privilege of representing Scotland at the World Cup finals because I had dreamed of doing so since I was a child. I trusted the governing body and the manager to look after us as best they could, but some of the Anglos held a different view, Manchester United's Lou Macari in particular. He made his feelings clear by saying something along the lines of he would be better off staying at home because he could make more money working at his chip shop outside Old Trafford. The three Aberdeen players who were present – Bobby Clark, Stuart Kennedy and me – were so disgusted that we got up and walked out. Bobby was particularly upset and remarked that it was shameful the players were arguing over a few hundred pounds when many Scotland fans would probably be spending their life-savings to travel to Argentina. I agreed with Bobby 100 per cent. If it had been up to me, Lou would have been told not to worry about the bonuses because he would not be on the plane. That was not Ally's style, though. He had also left it to the SFA to sort out the bonus levels, mainly through skipper Bruce Rioch. I do not think that Ally was aware the issue had still not been settled when we reached Argentina, and some players were continuing to nip his ears. Whatever, the SFA should have handled the matter in a professional way. When Ally became involved he argued that the squad should just get on with trying to qualify from our group and continue to argue with the SFA when their hands would be considerably stronger, thanks to their performances. But some players, mainly those based in England so far as I am concerned, wanted guarantees about money up-front, and it was annoying that Ally was having to deal with that so late in the day.

If memory serves me right, the deal agreed was something like £680 a man for being at the finals, the bonus rising if we moved on to the next stage, which was a fair return in 1978. A players' pool of finance raised by various advertising spin-offs would see each of us pocket about £8,000, so complaints were hardly justified.

Ally's optimism about our chances in Argentina was echoed by almost every punter in Scotland. He had stimulated the same effect at Aberdeen, almost as if the man could hypnotise football fans at times. Ally was like the Pied Piper as he told everyone what they wanted to hear, and the fans, in particular, were more than happy to go along with the positive vibes.

I doubt that any Scotland team generated as much interest as in the feverish lead-up to those finals when Ally did the round of television chat shows and radio stations, and was ubiquitous in spreading the word in newspapers too.

The manager was doing his job: can you imagine the reaction he would have stirred if he had said the Scotland squad were rubbish and had no chance at the finals? The SFA bought into the hype as well, so much so that they organised that embarrassing farewell parade at Hampden to give the Tartan Army a chance to wish their heroes good luck. The fans had to pay for the privilege, of course, and I know for a fact that was not Ally's idea. TV pictures of him walking down the red carpet onto the Hampden pitch showed that. Ally was normally the most demonstrative of men and Dons fans used to cheer when they saw him shooting out from the dug-out celebrating every goal in excited fashion. He knew how to milk the applause from an audience, but that day at Hampden Ally walked out with his head down and kept his hands in the pockets of his jacket. He was clearly embarrassed by the entire nonsense the SFA were forcing us to endure. It was the same for the players as we were taken around the Hampden pitch on an open-top bus. We had earned nothing so far, so we all felt a bit uneasy. Alan Rough at least lightened the mood by picking out the prettiest girls in the crowd and rating them out of 10.

We headed off to Prestwick Airport with fans lining the streets to wish us on our way. The country was caught up in a frenzy and I recall Ally turning and saying to me: 'Imagine what it's going to be like when we come back, if we do well.' To the delight of the players the SFA had booked first-class tickets for the long flight to South America. That lifted our spirits and we thought that if this was a sign of how intensively the SFA had worked to look after us, that the campaign would perhaps pan out as Ally hoped.

I remember little of the flight beyond the few minutes after take-off because I was suddenly struck down by terrible illness. I do not know to this day what the problem was, but I felt sick and at one stage feared I might be suffering a heart attack. The Scotland physician Doc Fitzsimmons considered that the occasion had simply proved too much for me and that I had been overwhelmed by the euphoria of the World Cup. He administered a couple of injections to help to calm me down and I slept like a baby for most of the flight. We reached Cordoba in Argentina 21 hours after leaving Scotland and were sent to an office at the airport where photographs were taken for our official passes. While we were waiting a representative of a major newspaper in the country asked if some of us would pose for press pictures, and Ally agreed. The photographer also persuaded a couple of air stewardesses and young women assistants from shops at the airport to enter the frame, and the Scotland players toasted them with glasses of cola and orange juice. The rest, including Ally, were looking on in amusement, but we did not laugh when a picture was published, but more of that in due course.

The SFA's plans to ensure that we travelled in style juddered to a halt thanks to the bus assigned to take us on to our training camp at Alta Gracia. It was ancient, but as we chugged off we noted that many of the people were living in slum conditions, often with bits of corrugated iron as their only shelter by the roadside. One thing that stuck in my mind was the bus driving past a dead horse lying in the road. When we returned on our way home six weeks later, it was still decaying away while children played nearby. We were given a tremendous welcome by the locals at Alta Gracia, and they had organised an Argentinean pipe band to accompany us from the town centre to our hotel. But at that point our poor bus had decided that enough was enough and thick black smoke began to spew from the engine and to engulf the passengers sitting inside. 'They are trying to kill us,' Alan Rough offered as a joke while we struggled for breath. (On our way home, Alan reminded me of the bus incident with: 'I wish they *had* killed us, Joe!').

Our hotel, the Sierras, looked fine from a distance. It was a sprawling white Spanish-style building set in massive grounds with an ornamental garden, and we were confident that it would provide a great place to stay for the next few weeks. Within a few days, I'm afraid, some of us had dubbed it Chateau Despair because it was so awful. The rooms were akin to school dormitories and we were squashed three men to each one. I shared with Alan Rough and Derek Johnstone which was a nightly trial. It was so hot that we slept naked and my bed was the middle one: if I turned one way during the night I would be met with the vision of a naked Alan, his pillow engulfed by his blond, curly perm, and if I adjusted my position the other way Derek's black, curly perm looked even worse. I reckon I earned a bonus on top of my bonus for putting up with that as well as coping with their constant pranks.

I must say that the mischief helped to take our minds off the dire living conditions. The food was poor and consisted mainly of a choice between horsemeat steaks and salad, which was not the most appetising fare in the stifling heat we had to contend with. At least they served ice-cream, which I consumed every day until I took a mouthful and told the lads that it was more delicious than usual thanks to the addition of some raisins. I had fallen for the prank: the added ingredient consisted of dead flies. Still, many of us got by on a diet of the Mars bars that the SFA had brought out to boost energy levels and a thin soup that the hotel served, which was tasty enough.

The accommodation was basic and run down and Martin Buchan joked that he always left the door to his room unlocked when he set off for training in the hope that someone might slip in to decorate the place. We guffawed when we were told that one Scottish newspaper had reported that we were living in 'opulent conditions with a golf course, heated swimming pool and tennis courts to help the players relax'. The pool came without water, the court had no net and if we wanted a game of golf we had to share one bag containing only eight clubs. The SFA had done their bit to try to enliven our existence in the evenings by arranging some videos for us to view: the collection comprised 12 titles to last us more than a month.

Armed guards swarmed all over the hotel complex and they were far more strict about letting us out than allowing visitors in, so we often bumped into fans who had evaded security simply because they were wearing kit with a player's name emblazoned on the back. We could escape only if we possessed a precious note from Ally to give to the guards, and we had to inform them of the exact time we would return. Players who were a few minutes over their allotted time were hunted down by armed guards. The manager permitted us to visit the casino that was part of the complex but was surrounded by a 3ft-high wall. Guards insisted that we leave the main gate and walk around the wall to reach the gambling joint, which was quite a detour, but some of the lads had the cheek to step over the low wall instead – and were immediately surrounded by guards pointing guns at them. When the negative publicity erupted later that audacious act was turned into stories claiming the lads were drunk, that they had scaled a 12ft fence and that they had been ordered to get down. I can assure the reader that did not happen.

The stirred-up scandal hurt to the core because Ally was particularly helpful to the press pack who had accompanied us to Argentina. He held a conference with them at 9.30 a.m. every day, which no other national manager had time for in those days. We discovered later that some reporters had used the extra access they were granted to sneak away and ask hotel staff if they had spotted any of the Scotland party getting drunk or committing acts of mischief. I asked Ally why he felt the need to speak to the press so early each day, and his reasoning was: 'The boys have jobs to do as well. It means they can keep their bosses happy by getting their stories over early and have the rest of the day free to enjoy themselves. They've always been good to me, so I don't mind helping them a bit.' The relationship would alter markedly.

The gentlemen of the press could at least get access to telephones to dictate their copy wherever they were staying. Telephones were not supplied in our rooms so we had to book slots with the hotel switchboard if we wanted to call our families back home. On one occasion it took three days for me to make contact with Fiona, so in the end most of us just gave up on the phone system. Boredom was the biggest enemy and a rope was extended across the tennis court as a makeshift net so that we could have a smashing time. Alan Rough and I almost came a cropper when we played a couple of the guards. It was clear that they were annoyed we were on top in the game and their rifles were lying nearby, so I told Alan it might be best if we just let them win, and to this day he winds me up about that being the only time he saw me happy to lose.

The SFA committee members had no worries about poor facilities 40 minutes away in their five-star hotel in Cordoba. I know that Ally complained about the conditions for the players, and he revealed to me that another hotel had been selected when he and Ernie Walker had visited Argentina on a fact-finding mission a few months before the finals. His pleas fell on deaf ears, but Ally did his best to hide his disappointment and worked even harder to keep the atmosphere in the camp as positive as possible. He organised bingo with Mars bars provided for the winners and staged competitive quizzes, but because he had no reference books to hand he made up the questions on the spot. Ally being Ally he often came up with the wrong answers which caused a few arguments, and he also liked to join one of the quiz teams from time to time. As he was setting the questions and providing the answers, no Mars bar for guessing which team won. Veteran Scotland physio Jim Steele did his best to lift spirits too, and queues formed at his room for a massage and the opportunity to hear some of his funny tales. Jimmy admitted that he had not come across conditions as bad as those we suffered in Argentina.

One aspect of the expedition that obviously kept us going day by day was training. Ally has been criticised for lack of pre-paration, but he and assistant John Hagarty were absolutely spot-on in Argentina in my opinion, though the training pitch was 30 minutes away from our hotel, and rutted and bare in places. Each session was varied and interesting with plenty of competitive games to add a bit of spice and fun to the proceed-ings. Ally and John *had* done their homework and prepared as much as they could to ensure that the squad were ready for the challenges ahead. But their dedication to the cause was about to be undone by a veteran Peruvian footballer called Teofilio Cubillas and a Scotsman by the name of Willie Johnston.

18

WOES AND A WIN IN ARGENTINA

'Friends that Ally thought populated the Scottish press had sharpened their pencils and their daggers'

Willie Johnston was not the only Scotland star to take illegal substances at the 1978 World Cup finals in Argentina. When Archie Gemmill made that claim a few years ago, severe criticism was directed at him by some other members of the ill-fated tour. Archie was telling the truth. The Reactivan tablets that Willie took – and which ultimately earned him a life-ban from international football – were in common use in England in the 1970s. I will not name the culprits I have in mind. It is for them to have the guts to come forward and admit they were guilty and that they were fortunate not to be chosen to provide a urine sample after the opening World Cup group match against Peru. Willie's woes overshadowed everything else that occurred, but I reckon that if Scotland's followers had been aware of the shambles that engulfed the build-up to the tournament, they might have offered a bit more sympathy.

We were certainly pleased to have a real game to worry about after enduring the poor conditions provided courtesy of the SFA. The game against Peru took place in Cordoba and almost to a man the Scottish press predicted an easy win for Ally MacLeod's men. The manager himself was far more cautious. Poor Ally bore the brunt of the blame for our 3-1 defeat afterwards because some players that he had been good enough to take with him pointed to his supposed lack of preparation and poor tactics. I have noted previously that tactics were not Ally's main strength, but the claim that he had not prepared for the biggest game in his managerial career is nonsense. Total nonsense.

Ally is on record as claiming that the destination of the World Cup could be decided by the quality of free-kicks taken during the tournament. He had identified the danger posed by balls being hit in the right way in hot and humid conditions. He backed up that assertion by warning us that it was important to set up our wall properly at set-pieces and he had prepared dossiers on Peru and the other nations we would face in our group, Iran and Holland. Thus former players suggesting that Scotland did not do well because he failed to provide ample warning about the challenges we faced are merely attempting to divert attention from their below-par displays. I can confirm that Ally did his best to convince his side that opponents were not so good as was the actual case. He adopted that ploy when he was the manager of Aberdeen, and it certainly served the purpose in getting us going against the Old Firm in particular. Ally talked of Peru's star men Teofilio Cubillas, Hector Chumpitaz and Hugo Sotil as being past it, and the words came back to haunt him, but he was attempting to convince his troops that they had nothing to fear. 'Treat them with respect, though, and we can win,' he added subtly. I reckon Scotland could have done just that.

Hindsight is wonderful, but I consider that Ally's biggest mistake was to stick with Don Masson and Bruce Rioch, who had given him great service but were not up to the extra demands of playing in midfield in Argentina. Archie Gemmill and Graeme Souness were not banging on the door for inclusion – they wanted to knock it down – and I continue to wonder how our fortunes might have turned if they had been the first choices from the outset in the team of '78. Years later I asked Ally if he agreed and he replied: 'I see your point, but I was trying to build up a club atmosphere in the squad, and you don't get that if you aren't loyal to the players who are loyal to you.' He paid a high price for his acts of loyalty, though we made the perfect start on the field when Joe Jordan pounced to score after the Peruvian goalkeeper had spilled the ball. Even when Peru equalised with Cueto finishing off a clever passing move, I felt confident that we would win, and we were offered a gilt-edged opportunity to regain the lead in the second half when Rioch was chopped down inside Peru's penalty-area. Masson's penalty attempt was saved, and if we had gone 2-1 up I am sure that the South Americans, who were under intense pressure at that stage, would have crumbled. Instead they took encouragement from Don's blunder, and it was time for Cubillas to show that he was still capable of a match-winning performance.

Ally kept shouting for Scotland to push the Peruvians as far up the park as possible, but they retreated and left Cubillas with time and space to curl an impressive 20-yard shot past Alan Rough. Ally responded by hauling off Masson and Rioch, but it was all over almost immediately afterwards when my Dons team-mate Stuart Kennedy conceded a free-kick just outside our penalty-area. Cubillas fashioned as fine a free-kick as I have witnessed live in curling the ball around Scotland's defensive wall and into the net. It was an unstoppable effort, and the crucifixion of Ally MacLeod loomed. He had a go in the dressing-room afterwards, demanding: 'How could you not turn up for a game like that?' Typically his rant culminated with an attempt to lift our spirits: 'Keep the heads up. We still have two games to go. We can still make the next round.'

At that point, however, the friends that Ally thought populated the Scottish press had sharpened their pencils and their daggers. They had filed reports slating him for picking the wrong team and tactics, and few observers blamed the players for simply failing to perform. The focus would soon move from the game itself.

❖

Those in the Scotland dressing-room paid little attention when Kenny Dalglish and Archie Gemmill were called through to provide urine that could be tested for drugs. Archie returned about five minutes later to say that FIFA officials had got the numbers mixed up and wanted Willie Johnston to provide a sample instead. So began one of the biggest scandals to rock the foundations of Scottish football. I have spoken to Willie many times over the years about what followed, and I maintain that he was treated very unfairly. He admitted up-front that he had taken the pills to combat hay fever. Willie honestly thought he was doing nothing wrong because the pills were in common use at his club, West Bromwich Albion, and throughout the English leagues. I also noticed some of the Anglo-Scots using nasal sprays, but these were not hard drugs, and the English FA were conducting drug tests by that time, so they clearly had no problem with the tablets that Willie was consuming. That said the SFA had warned us to be extra careful because FIFA were cracking down on players using illegal substances, but I can understand why the Anglos thought they would not be facing problems.

Willie duly gave his sample, and we went off to prepare for a reception organised by the British Embassy and hosted by the Minister for Sport, Denis Howell, in a Cordoba hotel. By the time we got there we could sense something was up, because Ally was very tense and it was noticeable that he was conducting private chats with SFA officials. Matters came to a head when

Trevor McDonald, then a reporter for ITV, attempted to corner Willie for an interview. Ally, who had always been willing to co-operate with the press, lost his patience and exclaimed: 'There is a time and a place to interview players and it is during the day, not when we are here [with representatives of] the British Embassy.' Ally, who had granted McDonald and his film crew access to the reception in the first place, added: 'You're pushing your luck. I never thought there would come a day when I would have to ask you to leave. You are stooping to low tactics.'

The press and broadcasting media had been alerted before we knew details of the Willie Johnston crisis, and next morning he woke to find scores of reporters from many countries camped outside his hotel room. Willie was taken into a meeting with Ally and confessed that he had swallowed two tablets. He was also confronted by the mighty figures of the SFA and whisked away from our camp hidden under a jacket in the back of a car. Willie was driven on an eight-hour journey to Buenos Aires and he was flown to London via Rio de Janeiro and Paris. The Scotland players still had not been told that he had departed! When Ally finally held a meeting to deliver the news, we all felt bad on behalf of Willie and the Scotland set-up in general. But I believe it was wrong that the SFA did not at least give Willie the chance to state his case properly; he was hung out to dry and not allowed to explain that those pills were in common use at his club.

As you might expect, Ally ordered us to make sure that we handed over any medicines, anonymously if required, and he admitted that he was shocked by the amount of stuff collected. This produced a standing joke that he threw the bag of pills and other medicines out of the bus window into a field of cows while we were heading for training, and when we were on the return journey we saw the cows doing back-flips and hand-stands. Not true, but it was Ally's way of trying to lift spirits, though he did not hide the fact that the situation was serious.

I can reveal here that three other Scotland players ran the risk of being banned for taking substances deemed illegal by FIFA after Willie had gone home. I was one of them. Alan Rough, Derek Johnstone and I were resting in our room discussing how Willie had been treated when Doc Fitzsimmons walked in. He spotted a Vicks nasal spray lying on a bedside table and almost went berserk. 'Who the fu** is using that?' asked the Doc, who was so angry that I feared the veins on the side of his head would pop. Derek had developed a heavy cold and had bought the medication to clear his nose, and Alan and I had also used it because the vapours helped to moisten our nostrils after training. It did not cross our minds that a problem could arise, but the Doc pointed to the ingredients, a few of which were included on the FIFA blacklist.

It was just as well that did not leak out at the time, because the press had declared open season on Ally and the squad. We heard that one Scottish reporter, Fraser Elder, was wandering about the village with pictures of squad members and inquiring if anyone had seen them breaking curfews or drinking heavily. That was confirmed by locals who worked at the hotel and were disgusted by what was going on. Elder eventually got his just desserts when Rangers' Tam Forsyth, not one to be messed with, ran into him. Tam's wife was pregnant and he was furious about much of the coverage appearing in Scotland, so he grabbed Elder by the throat and threatened to kill him. Tam would probably have been obliged to wait in a queue to pursue his threat.

Given all that was going on it was hard for the squad to focus their minds on the forthcoming tie against Iran. Clearly the strain was telling on Ally, but he did his best to disguise it with the message: 'Stick together lads. We can still get through.' As subsequent World Cups have shown, there is no such thing as a bad team when you get to the final stages of the competition.

Iran may have been unfamiliar to us, but they were not so bad as the media had made out, and we failed to deliver once more. Ally MacLeod's fate was sealed and I take my share of the blame because I played for the closing 13 minutes of the Iran match. It saddens me to recall that I was not at my best when given the opportunity to fulfil the dream that had been stimulated by grainy black-and-white TV images of Pele performing at the finals in Sweden 20 years before. It was a poor game in Cordoba, though we experienced a lucky break just before half-time when Andranik Eskandarian scored a daft own-goal when he was put under pressure by Joe Jordan. Iraj Danaei-Fard's equaliser came via a shot from a tight angle that sneaked past Alan Rough at his front post. I was confident that I could emulate *Roy of the Rovers* and save Scotland when I replaced the injured Kenny Dalglish.

I picked out Sandy Jardine with a 30-yard pass to his feet, but thereafter hardly registered a touch because we were so desperate that the plan was limited to kicking high balls towards Joe Jordan in the hope that he would score from one. We forced a sequence of corner-kicks in the last minute, so they had two men marking big Joe. I kept telling him to take them to the front post and leave a bit of extra space for me when the ball came in, but Joe ignored me and continued to go for every cross. The ball fell at my feet late on, but their penalty-box was so packed with defenders it was scrambled clear before I got a shot in.

When the final whistle sounded I just wished that the ground would open up and swallow me, for this was not how my World Cup story was supposed to end. The Tartan Army, who had spent personal fortunes to reach Argentina, reacted with fury, but some went too far. Fans situated above the tunnel as we made our way off the pitch began to spit on us and my hair and shirt displayed the evidence. I suppose that verbal abuse, even extreme examples of personal insults, could be tolerated in the circumstances, but the individuals who spat on us could not be forgiven. I was tempted to clear the wall and to seek revenge and I would not have been alone among my team-mates, but I felt even worse when I reached the safety of the dressing-room. Scotland's one-time cheerleader Ally MacLeod had deteriorated into a shell that was totally broken. He was devastated and speechless, in the latter state probably for the first time since I had met him. He did not need to utter a word for we knew that we had let him down and the Scottish nation as well. The outbreak of spitting continued even after we had boarded the bus to extricate us from the stadium, and I have never felt as heartsick after a football match as I did on that fateful day.

The media now had more than enough ammunition to destroy Ally, and they did not seem to care how they went about it. Our fury and frustration intensified when we picked up the local paper and saw displayed on the front page the picture that had been snapped on our arrival in Argentina weeks before. A hotel receptionist translated and left us stunned by relaying the paper's claim that the picture showed Scotland players partying with local girls and drinking Bacardis and Coke the night before the Iran game. Worse, some Scottish papers carried the picture and the bogus story despite the fact that members of the home press corps had been present at the airport when it was taken. Ally urged us to ignore the media nonsense, which proved difficult, especially when we were still asked to wait up to three days to contact our families by phone. I asked TV commentator Archie Macpherson, who was one of the few from the media who had not turned on us, to phone my wife the next time he visited the press centre to let her know I was okay. He did me the favour. Bobby Clark was particularly upset to learn that his wife had taken a call from a stranger ranting about his supposed drinking and partying in Argentina, which was arrant nonsense because my colleague was a thoroughly dedicated and clean-living professional. Some 10 minutes later his wife received a call from a journalist asking for her comment on rumours that she had been informed about what Bobby was getting up to in Argentina. Perverse!

Ally did his plucky best to buck us up, but it was an impossible task by that stage. The final straw came when he managed to sneak us away from the mayhem to watch Mexico play West Germany in their final group game.

The Mexicans, who lost 5-0, were staying at our hotel and Ally decided that it would be a good idea to let us relax and enjoy some beers with them after they returned. We enjoyed ourselves for once and wished the Mexicans well when they set off for home the next day, but if we had laid hands on their coach a few hours later we might have lynched him. The local paper, making mischief once more, carried a front-page story and the word '*Escotia*' caught the eye. The article was based on an interview with the Mexican coach, who blamed the Scotland players and officials for contributing to their poor performances at the finals because the group were kept awake by us running along hotel corridors late at night chasing naked women and drinking whisky. I deny the lurid tale and certainly after the 1975 goings-on in Copenhagen, the lifetime ban that was lifted and my recall for international duty, I was determined to avoid trouble of any kind in Argentina.

Many of us would have opted to take the next flight home because we were under siege, press photographers and reporters seemed to be cropping up everywhere and there seemed little hope of us preparing properly for our final match against the Dutch, though we still had an outside chance of qualifying for the next round. Graeme Souness, at 25 one of the younger members of the squad, stepped forward to demonstrate the qualities that would make him an outstanding Scotland captain and successful Rangers manager. The players held a meeting at which Archie Gemmill worked hard to remind us that we could

still regain some pride, and Graeme weighed in with the speech
that got everyone going again. He spoke from the heart about
the unfortunate happenings so far, but stressed that we could
rescue something from disaster if we stuck together and used the
factors that had been threatening to tear Scotland apart to unite
us for one last effort – to show the world that we could play
football. I felt a lump in my throat when Graeme said we owed it
to Ally to go out and beat the Dutch regardless of whether
victory would be enough to get us through to the next stage. Our
target was to beat them by three clear goals and then Scotland
and Peru would advance. (We were not aware that FIFA had
already decided we would have points deducted and be elimi-
nated as part of our punishment for Willie's misdemeanour.)

You could sense the mood in our camp had changed for the
better, so it is little surprise that we outplayed Holland, who
went all the way to the grand final. Inevitably our game is
recalled most for Archie Gemmill's wonderful goal, which is
perhaps the best scored by a Scotland player, but I prefer to
remember a match from which an entire nation regained some
pride and which gave Ally the chance to stick two farewell
fingers up at people he had treated as friends, but who had
turned on him in ways that were inexcusable. For his part Ally
showed steely determination that day and ordered SFA hangers-
on from our bus before delivering his final pre-match speech as
Scotland manager. He read out his team and list of substitutes,
then said: 'Right, let's go and fu****g play. It's our last game,
let's show all those bastards what you are made of.' Ally had
little need to say anything else.

We went behind to a penalty, but then showed the fighting
spirit that had taken us to Argentina in the first place. Kenny

Dalglish equalised and then Souness, who was magnificent, was chopped down for a penalty. Archie converted the award, then proceeded on his distinctive dance through the Dutch defence, and suddenly it was 3-1 and Scotland were a goal short of glory. The joy lasted just three minutes until Johnny Rep struck a stunning long-distance shot past Alan Rough, but those amounted to the most wonderful three minutes of the entire trip.

It was glorious failure nonetheless, so the long journey home was grim mainly because we knew the carping and criticism would continue long after the culmination of the 1978 World Cup finals. The Anglo-Scots proved to be the lucky ones for they broke away when we arrived in London, while a small group including Ally, Derek Johnstone, Alan Rough, Stuart Kennedy and myself travelled on to Glasgow. We could see that fans had turned out in force at the airport, but none of us wished to be first off the plane, so Alan Rough shouted towards Ally: 'Look boss, they've sent out a welcoming party.' Ally knew the proper score, but exited with his head held high and waved at the fans as they pelted us with abuse. Our bus was mobbed by so-called supporters when it left the airport: they covered the windows with spittle and bayed for our blood.

Playing for my country was one of my proudest achievements, but I would most probably have declined if I had been offered another opportunity to represent Scotland at the World Cup. What a load of life's nonsense we had to endure as a result of the Argentina fiasco, but it continues to upset me that because of our shortcomings at the finals, Ally tends to be remembered as a bit of a joke as a manager. Believe me when I say that his memory deserves a lot better than that, which is why I was delighted to learn in 2008 that a group of Ayr United fans had put his name forward for a place in Scotland's Hall of Fame at Hampden. My delight turned to disgust when Craig Brown, one of his successors, was quoted as saying that Ally did not deserve to be honoured in that way. 'I love Ally and he was a major personality in Scottish football, but I don't think you can say in terms of achievement that he deserves to be there,' said Brown, and my respect for him evaporated immediately. Curious that the Scotland team managed by Craig Brown at the 1998 World Cup finals in France were hailed as heroes when they came home, though they did not win any of their three games and finished with a 3-0 mauling by Morocco. Ally MacLeod, despite horrendous problems, most of which were far beyond his control, did better than that . . . The world of football can be extremely cruel.

19

DEALING WITH FERGIE

'You better get used to not being in the team'

I do not wish to speak to Sir Alex Ferguson ever again. At one time I agonised over why we failed to hit it off after he became manager of Aberdeen Football Club in the summer of 1978. I had just returned from a nightmare spell with Scotland in Argentina and was eager to return to my club and to impress the new boss. I scored 33 goals for Aberdeen in Fergie's first season, but unfortunately it was clear to me from the early stages of his managership that he had it in for me.

I wish I could pinpoint the reason and one of the theories goes that he was jealous of the great rapport that I enjoyed with the Aberdeen supporters. No man is bigger than the club and I certainly did not believe that I was, but I cannot help wondering if Fergie considered my hero status as some sort of threat to his authority. That thought crossed my mind years later when I noted how he got rid of David Beckham at Manchester United at a time when the 'Posh and Becks' phenomenon was at its height. Beckham had become the main man at Old Trafford in the eyes of the fans and the media, and he was soon moved on. I am no David Beckham, but I was a massive favourite with the Aberdeen support and a senior figure at Pittodrie. Also I would hate to think that he had carried forward some resentment from the time I stole his thunder when we travelled with a Scotland squad on the world tour that took in Hong Kong, Down Under and elsewhere. Whatever the reason, Alex Ferguson, who was only 36 when he took charge at Pittodrie, seemed to see me as a threat rather than an asset. The view was mistaken, for all that I wished to do was to play football and to score goals, preferably for Aberdeen. I did not need to be on friendly terms with my manager to carry that through, and yet I did not seek to create conflict with any of my gaffers. Why should I?

I often wondered about asking for a meeting with Fergie so that we could talk things through and figure out why our relationship was so bad. Any desire to take that course vanished when Fergie's autobiography, *Managing My Life*, was published in 1999. When I studied the passages that referred to me, I felt a strong desire to burn the book. I was particularly upset by the section describing his meeting the Aberdeen players for the first time:

'The only individual who seemed to present a long-term problem was the little front man, Joe Harper. Joe was a hero with the fans, but for me, whether he was on his two legs or on four wheels, he was a worry. I had misgivings about him as early as pre-season training, when I found myself lapping him during an endurance run (three-and-a-half years after I had stopped playing seriously). The suspicion that he was an artful dodger was strengthened one day when he stopped me outside the back door of the dressing-rooms to tell me how much the players were enjoying my coaching. "We never got any coaching when Big Billy was here," he informed me. I have no time for such nonsense, and Harper's motives for peddling it were exposed the following week when he came to me with a request for a testimonial.

'I marked him down as somebody to watch. Apparently the local constabulary did the same. Not long after taking over, my phone rang in the small hours and the police told me they were holding Joe on a drink-driving charge, and asked if I would accept his call. He wasn't exactly incoherent, but his plea was madness: "Will you please contact the Chief Constable, Alex Morrison, and see if they will drop this charge? I've only had three pints."

Alex Ferguson claimed that he then called Dons vice-chairman Chris Anderson, who told him to ignore my alleged plea and go back to sleep. Fergie added: 'Soon afterwards, having received another call from the police station telling me Joe was two-and-a-half times over the limit, I did.'

I was infuriated by all this. Allow me to state my case. I have openly admitted that I was never a fan of long-distance running, but I have no recollection of Fergie lapping me on the training pitch. I categorically deny saying anything disparaging about Billy McNeill, who is now a close friend and was a brilliant coach and manager at Aberdeen. The comment about the testimonial is fabrication so far as I am concerned. The club agreed to award me the testimonial as part of the new contract I signed when Billy was still boss at Pittodrie. I certainly did not call Fergie in an effort to persuade him to get a drink-driving charge dropped. I was prosecuted for driving while over the limit, something of which I have always been deeply ashamed. But given how quickly our relationship had deteriorated at Pittodrie, Alex Ferguson was the last man I would have called to help me in a difficult situation. I *did not* make the telephone call he mentioned in his book. I considered taking legal action over the contents, but how could I prove anything? Chris Anderson, who would have been able to confirm if the telephone conversation took place or did not take place, died in 1986.

It's down to Fergie's word against mine, and I must say that it did not surprise me that others, including Gordon Strachan and Jim Leighton, disputed other claims made in the book. Going by what he wrote, though, Fergie really hated me, yet I cannot recall being negative in any way when he took the reins at Pittodrie. Like the rest of the Dons players, I did my best to respond in the manner that he wanted.

❖

The Aberdeen players were excited to a man when Alex Ferguson held a meeting and spoke of his desire to field a team that would play exciting, attacking football and beat the Old Firm to trophies on a regular basis.

We were sold on him from day one, and I cannot recall giving the manager any cause to think that I was not fully committed. He was a young manager so he encountered a few teething problems, and one habit that got our backs up was his comparing Aberdeen players with those he had previously managed at St Mirren. Commenting on a Willie Miller move at training or in a match, Fergie would say: 'Jackie Copeland would have done it this way.' He made similar comparisons between Gordon Strachan and Tony Fitzpatrick and Frank McAvennie and myself. I was not the only one who was annoyed by such remarks. Willie Miller and Jackie Copeland? No comparison. Willie, as strong a character as Alex Ferguson and the ideal candidate for captain, eventually sorted things out. He met Fergie to point out that the St Mirren comparisons were causing friction, and they stopped.

We made a great start to the 1978-79 league campaign and were undefeated after five games. I scored seven times and was doing what I could to show Fergie that I was eager to figure in his inspiring plans. I believe, though, that a rift opened up when we lost 2-1 at Hibs in our sixth league match. As promised, we had engaged in attacking football in the first five games and had blown Hearts away by 4-1 in our encounter at Tynecastle, but the manager surprised us by changing to a 4-5-1 formation for the fixture at Easter Road, fielding me as lone striker and dropping Steve Archibald back into midfield. I roomed with Steve at our Edinburgh hotel the night before the game, and he admitted that he was worried because he was unsure of the role he was being asked to fulfil. Steve hardly slept a wink, and it was no surprise that he did not perform efficiently at Easter Road. I felt that I had done well enough as the sole striker, but I am sure we could have taken points from the game if we had stuck to the formation that had brought us so much success. We analysed our performance while travelling on the bus back to Aberdeen – Fergie was not with us because he and his wife were still resident in Glasgow – and we agreed that we had not played well, but also felt that the change in tactics had not worked out.

This was the first Ferguson defeat as Aberdeen manager and we were suitably curious to see how he would react. Come the Monday we were ordered to sit in the centre circle of the Pittodrie pitch and to wait for him. He announced his arrival by storming out of the tunnel cursing and swearing at the top of his voice, and he did not let up until he reached us, roaring: 'Right, you bunch of useless bastards, we will sort this out now. What do you think went wrong?' We reacted in the way that most players tend towards in such a situation by staring at the ground to avoid eye contact as Fergie ranted on. I had seen it all before when Eddie Turnbull was in charge, and to make any comment at that time would have been courting personal dis-aster. I was forced to look up, however, when Fergie demanded: 'Harper, what do you think went wrong?' He had asked me directly, so I responded with an honest answer: 'I don't think the tactics worked, boss.' Asked what I meant by that, I explained that we had found it difficult to adapt and I mentioned how Steve was so worried that he hardly slept during the night before the game.

Now Alex Ferguson did not lose the head at this point. He listened and scouted around the group seeking opinions. I was impressed by the way he had considered everyone's views and I thought that was the end of the post-mortem. After the training session, however, Teddy Scott informed me that the manager wanted to see me in his office. I did not consider the business would be serious, so I was shocked when I walked in and Fergie shouted: 'Bloody sit down.' He jabbed a finger and challenged me: 'Who do you think you are to question my tactics?' The more Fergie remonstrated with me the more his stabbing finger closed on my face. I eventually grabbed the digit and shouted: 'Don't you ever point a finger at me like that again. I was brought up to show good manners, and I would never do that to anyone. I'm not paid to manage the club, but you asked for my opinion and I gave an honest answer. If you don't want my opinion, don't ask for it.' I stormed out of his office, and our relationship became increasingly frosty from that day on, but it did not alter the effort that I expended for our manager in training or in matches.

It is well documented that Fergie can be a bit of a bully, particularly when it comes to dealing with younger players, and he also likes to show that he is in control of the senior figures. He took things a little too far after we had been invited to film a *New Year Party* special for Grampian Television, the station based in Aberdeen. Specials were prepared in advance, so it felt strange to be dressed up in kilts and faking the festive atmosphere. Fergie was invited with Bobby Clark, Alan Rough, Stuart Kennedy and me, and Charlie Rettie, a local hotelier who was also a Grampian guest, invited us to a genuine party at his house after the recording. Fergie walked into the kitchen where my wife and I were talking to other folk and I was about to tuck into haggis, neeps and tatties off a paper plate. 'What do you think you are doing?' he said. 'You have a weight problem, you can't eat that.' He snatched the plate and contents and threw the lot into the sink. I was furious because I felt it was neither the time nor the place to attempt to show me who was boss. I picked up another plate and heaped on a double portion, then made as if to scoff it. Alex Ferguson just glared at me and stormed out. I did not eat the food and had not intended to do so, but most people in the kitchen felt that his conduct was out of order.

The stage had been reached that the manager spoke to me only if necessary. I did not question the man's authority in public again, but played on, hoping that club matters would resolve themselves. Certainly no problems arose on the pitch apart from during a visit to Bulgaria where we were drawn to face Marek Dimitrov in the European Cup-Winners' Cup. Our centre-half Willie Garner suffered a broken leg and the injury was so serious that an ambulance had to drive onto the pitch before he could be removed. The game was held up for 15 minutes, and Willie told us later that he was horrified when he arrived at hospital to be thrown onto a big stone slab to await treatment. Bulgaria may have developed into a popular holiday destination, but some of its facilities were pretty backward in 1978. Staff eventually applied a plaster to the injured leg, but too tightly, and the club doctor later required to snip off bits of the dressing to ease the pressure and ensure that blood would reach Willie's toes. West German club Fortuna Dusseldorf knocked us out in the following round, but Fergie expressed confidence that we would learn from the experience for the next time we played in Europe.

We did have a chance to lift silverware to mark Fergie's first season in charge when we reached the Scottish League Cup final for the third season in succession. We were fortunate to see off Hibs at Dens Park in the semi-final, Stuart Kennedy claiming the only goal with a sliced cross that rose to great heights and plunged into the net as it descended. Stuart was a marvellous defender, but crossing the ball was not his strong point; still, his odd effort was welcome enough. We met Rangers in the final, and it was one of the most controversial showdowns in the history of the competition.

Duncan Davidson put us ahead though we were making a poor show of it, and Alex MacDonald equalised for Rangers. It was a tough tussle which exploded near the end when Doug Rougvie was sent off for allegedly striking my Argentina roommate Derek Johnstone. Referee Iain Foote missed what happened, but ordered big Doug off on the word of a linesman.

I saw it all clear as day. Doug and Derek collided as they went for a high ball, then fell to the turf. No punches were thrown nor did I notice flying elbows in what was a fair challenge for the ball involving two sturdy individuals, but Derek went down as if he had been struck by an express train. It seemed certain to me that the referee was about to take drastic action, so I rushed over to where Derek was laid out receiving treatment and pleaded: 'Come on big man, help Doug out here. He is about to get sent off.' Derek looked up at me, and smiled. Then Rangers full-back Sandy Jardine intervened and hauled me away from Derek by grabbing a handful of my hair. Sandy scampered off behind a posse of team-mates before I had the chance to retaliate by throwing a punch, and his speedy retreat meant that only one Aberdeen player received his marching orders that day.

We all felt sorry for Doug, who has always denied doing anything wrong. I have asked Derek frequently if he was actually hit, and he reacts predictably: he smiles nicely and offers a look at his winners' medal any time I want. Rangers won 2-1 thanks to an injury-time goal from Colin Jackson, and Doug, Bobby Clark and I were censured by the SFA for criticising the referee's ordering-off decision. But there is no doubt that Aberdeen were unfairly treated in that final appearance.

Hibs gained revenge by beating us in a Scottish Cup semifinal, and we eventually fell out of the title race and finished in fourth place, eight points behind champions Celtic. I scored in our last game, a 2-1 win over Partick Thistle at Firhill, to take my tally to 33 goals in all competitions. Fergie responded by taking me into a meeting to tell me that my days as an Aberdeen player were numbered. 'You better get used to not being in the team,' he announced, leaving me speechless. I had just completed a season as Scotland's top scorer ahead of Morton's Andy Ritchie, so I was obviously confident that I still had plenty to offer Aberdeen, and I could add to that goal tally the 55 I had amassed for the Dons in the previous two seasons. I was tempted to react by requesting a transfer, but then I wished to continue playing for Aberdeen.

Despite our personal differences, I was sure that Alex Ferguson would help to lead us to a Scottish League Championship, the achievement for which I yearned most. Not for the first time in my professional career, I decided that the best policy was to keep my head down and to hope that the flow of goals would make it difficult for the manager to overlook me. It proved to be the right decision because I completed a full set of domestic honours in season 1979-80, though I played only a bit-part in the production of Aberdeen's first title since 1955. Despite Fergie's warning that my days at Pittodrie were numbered, I gradually forced myself into his plans once more and was pleased to chip in with seven goals as we enjoyed a promising start in the league and marched into the quarter-finals of the League Cup. The seventh strike came in a 2-2 draw with St Mirren at Love Street on 6 October 1979.

It proved to be my 205th top-team goal for the Dons. And my last. My season ended when I suffered a serious knee injury during the second act of our League Cup quarter-final against Celtic in Glasgow on 24 November. Some Dons fans blame

Danny McGrain for making a wild tackle, mainly because they saw me try to punch the Celtic skipper as I fell to the turf.

Danny did nothing untoward. The injury had been caused earlier when I fell over another Celtic player Alan Sneddon. I felt acute pain in my right knee, far worse than experienced with previous knocks, though Dons physio Rolland Arnott decided that it was not as bad as I had feared and told me to carry on for a bit to check if the discomfort would ease. Five minutes later I was standing just in front of Danny waiting for a corner-kick to be played in. Danny's knee touched the back of my right leg ever so slightly, but it was enough to send me tumbling like a ton of bricks. Excruciating! And I was so sure that Danny had hit me that I tried to turn and punch him on the nose as I fell. I suffered the added indignity of being booked by the referee while being carried off on a stretcher in severe pain. I had to apologise to Danny later because he was an innocent party.

The cruciate ligaments in my knee had ruptured, and I was operated on at St John's Hospital in Aberdeen. The surgeon adjudged that the damage was not too bad and removed a bit of torn cartilage; I was assured that I would be back in training within six weeks, which proved to be right. Disaster struck, though, when I took part in a one-versus-one drill with Jim Leighton, who was then Aberdeen's reserve goalkeeper. The idea was to try to score, and as I attempted to jink past Jim my right leg went completely. I knew instantly that this *was* serious, and I was sent to a specialist in Harley Street, London, for more surgery. I was told that my knee was so badly damaged that I might not play football again. I was determined to disprove that idea despite spending the next three months with the leg encased in plaster and the knee bent, which made it almost impossible to move about. When the plaster was removed I was asked to try a simple exercise which involved lifting the right foot while balancing a small bean bag on top of it. I could not summon enough strength in the leg to complete that basic task, but I refused to throw in the towel and spent hour after hour at the Pittodrie gymnasium working on my general fitness. That regime lasted for more than a year, and it saddens me to relate that Alex Ferguson did not come in even once to ask how I was progressing. Not one word passed between us during that time.

Aberdeen clinched the league title in May 1980 with a 5-0 triumph over Hibs at Easter Road. I should have been delighted, but I was more concerned with the battle to regain fitness, and the disgraceful manner in which I was eventually 'presented' with a winners' medal (explained in the opening chapter) added to my frustration. Despondency eased a little when the Dons faced a select side in my testimonial match in August 1980: Aberdeen won 8-6. More than 14,000 fans turned out at Pittodrie, and taking a bow in front of them proved to be an emotional interlude, particularly as I was still hobbling around on crutches. Fergie penned a glowing tribute in my testimonial brochure, though what he wrote about me in 1999 suggested that those words of praise and encouragement were merely a sham.

There was no doubt that the cheers resounding from the Dons fans were genuine and they boosted my determination to get fully fit and to knock in goals for them again, though I realised that my chances of regaining the job of first-choice striker were slim. Mark McGhee, who went on to play for Hamburg and Celtic, was now the main marksman, and John Hewitt and Eric Black were pushing for recognition. I would have been happy to act as back-up to them, and at least I could offer advice. John Hewitt was an outstanding find and it delighted me that he progressed and scored the crucial goal against Real Madrid in the 1983 European Cup-Winners' Cup final. While John was a natural goal-scorer, a succession of managers insisted on him playing wide, and there is no doubt that if he had been cast as a striker more often my record tally of 205 goals would have been under threat. John's best pal at the time was a young midfielder, Neale Cooper, who had watched or joined our training since he was a lad at primary school. Neale's father had died so we took him under our wings, and he acted as a ball-boy and helped Teddy Scott to clear up after each training session. As Neale grew he joined us for kick-abouts, and we had no doubt that he would eventually mature into a fine player for Aberdeen. Neale also featured in the victory over Real Madrid and proved to be a key man in most of the club's achievements in the 1980s. I have become close to John and Neale in recent years, and they remain a credit to themselves and their families.

With so much talent available, I knew that Aberdeen Football Club were at the start of an exciting new era with Alex Ferguson in charge, and I wanted to be involved in the action even if that meant playing a bit-part. I reached the light at the end of the tunnel when I was declared fit to face Kilmarnock reserves at Pittodrie on 14 March 1981. It was stunning that 2,700 fans turned out for the reserve game, 200 more than were counted in to watch the first team lose 1-0 at Rugby Park the same afternoon. I was astonished by the reception from the Dons fans – it was gratifying that they had not forgotten me – and I responded by scoring a goal and setting up a few others as we hammered Killie's second string by a margin of 10-2.

I continued to work diligently in training and played a few more reserve games, and I was delighted when Fergie recalled me for the ultimate league game of 1980-81, also against Kilmarnock, at Pittodrie. We lost 2-0, but I saw selection for the senior team as a positive sign and still hoped that I would be retained when my contract expired that summer. The comments in the Ferguson biography make it clear that my optimism was sadly misplaced. The reign of the King of the Beach End was over.

20

A STROKE OF FORTUNE

'Lying in a hospital bed left time for much soul-searching'

Life after a playing career is tough when a man has been used to the excitement generated by big crowds, the camaraderie and a guaranteed standard of living. It saddens me to relate that my marriage fell victim to the difficulties that I experienced in adjusting to an altered regime. I found it hard to gain new-found job satisfaction, and I must admit that I became increasingly difficult to live with. Without going into too much personal detail, I can say that Fiona and I simply fell out of love during a painful part of our lives. We split in 1991 and she moved back to Glasgow, which proved difficult, especially for our son Ross and daughters Laura and Joanna. I must stress that not having a profession to fall back on beyond football was a major factor in my predicament, and it pleases me that nowadays the major clubs ensure that their trainee professionals are involved in some form of higher education, so that they can attain qualifications. My message to those young men is to devote as much attention to their studies as they do to football: they will be grateful that they have other skills to offer once their playing days are over.

Despite the failure of my marriage, I was ultimately able to piece together a meaningful 'life after football', and indeed was more fortunate than some others who had devoted their lives and souls to the game. I was obviously keen to continue in football in some way after my time as an Aberdeen player ended in the summer of 1981, so I went straight to Peterhead, who were then in the Highland League, as their player-manager. I scored 17 goals to help the Blue Toon finish runners-up in the league, but was then told that the club could not afford to keep paying me. I offered to take a cut in wages, but they said it would still be too costly, so that was that. Farewell. I also managed Deveronvale and Huntly and played for Keith for a spell. I enjoyed the Highland League, which is full of great characters such as Keith chairman Sandy Stables, a wonderfully jovial figure who certainly makes visitors welcome at their ground, Kynoch Park.

Football involvement was part-time, so I chose to work in the hotel and pub trade. I helped to run Joey Harper's, a bar in Union Street, Aberdeen, and learned the ropes as a waiter at the Amatola Hotel, then became general manager of the Earls Court Hotel, which is now a block of executive flats. I could not stay away from football, however. In 1987 I had a crack at managing in the junior ranks with the now defunct Rosslyn Sports, and also dabbled in youth coaching. It was never the same, though. Aberdeen are my club, and I could never really put my heart and soul into the job with any other outfit.

In 1989 I was involved in a crash while travelling as a passenger in a friend's car on the Aberdeen to Tarland road. Our Ford Orion was in collision with a Range Rover and somersaulted across the road onto its roof. My pal George Taylor and I were fortunate to suffer only minor bruises, but another passenger, Roy Brodie, broke his hip. The driver of the other vehicle was unhurt. George's car was written off, so we counted that as a lucky escape.

Thoughts of being involved in football again were behind me by then, and I was prepared for a happy retirement to feed off the host of happy memories I retain from my two spells at Pittodrie. My relationship with the Dons, which had been so badly soured when Alex Ferguson was in charge, gradually improved, and I was delighted when the club eventually invited me back to act as a host in one of the Pittodrie lounges on match days. The invitation to pen a column for the Aberdeen *Evening Express* was also readily accepted, though my comments have caused me problems from time to time, and I boosted my income with fees from after-dinner speaking. This was certainly not an activity that I had planned to undertake after speaking for the first time in public at my testimonial dinner in 1980. I had been terrified by that prospect and had no idea what to say, but journalist Andy Melvin came to my rescue by writing down a few jokes and creating some funny stories based upon my career. I had no intention of addressing other gatherings, but about four months after my dinner I received a phone call from a representative of a social club at Hurlford, near Kilmarnock. He had attended my testimonial, and he had concluded that I was a professional speaker! I was reluctant to speak at Hurlford, but I was per-suaded to give it a go. That first night I was panic-stricken, but I was able to make use of material from Andy which had been surplus to requirements at the Joe Harper dinner, and my speech went down well with the discerning Ayrshire audience. I was up and running on the after-dinner circuit.

As the years passed I was able to take such engagements in my stride, and I no longer feel nervous when called to the micro-phone, though speeches do not always turn out as planned. Take Lossiemouth Bowling Club, for instance. I was in agony because of an attack of gout, and my new partner Sheila had to be called upon to drive me northwards from Aberdeen because I did not wish to let the hosts down by not appearing. I was disappointed that only 23 diners were present and offered to forgo my fee and to travel back home, but the organisers insisted that the show had to go on. The audience were mostly veteran bowlers and clearly not interested in football, so I died a gout-ridden death. It's mostly fun, though, and I particularly enjoyed visiting Dubai to speak to a group of exiled Dons supporters. The trip was organised by Jim Geddie, boss of Apex (Aberdeen's shirt sponsors for 2005-08). He informed the exotic gathering that a Middle Eastern sheikh was guest of honour for the night – and he arranged for me to walk in with my identity obscured by traditional Arabian garb and sunglasses. Uproar ensued when the King of the Beach End revealed his true, majestic persona.

Travelling extensively to speak at dinners or other sporting events took its toll. I tended to arrive home in the early hours of the morning and began to put on a bit of weight, and my family expressed concern about my health. I brushed their comments aside, believing that ill-health was something that happened to other people, and received a rude awakening when asked to address a dinner at Kennoway Bowling Club in Fife in October of 2004.

I met the other speakers, former referee Brian McGinlay and ex-Rangers player Davie Wilson, and certainly did not feel any different that evening. I had been on my feet for about seven minutes when the microphone slipped out of my hand and fell to the floor. I bent down to pick it up, stood up to start speaking again – and was shocked to find that the mic was not in my hand. I looked down again and could have sworn I took a hold of it, but when I stood up again it still was not in my grasp. I recall hearing Brian McGinlay asking if I was okay, and the audience starting to laugh as I bent down to try to pick up the microphone for a third time. The laughter gained in volume as I struggled, the listeners assuming it was all a part of my act. Fortunately a paramedic was among the members of the audience, and he detected that something was seriously wrong. He called for a chair, and by the time I was helped to sit down I could feel the right side of my face was starting to droop. I felt my right arm weaken, and my right leg went as well. I thought I said: 'I'm okay', but Brian told me later that the words came out as a garbled noise. I felt no pain, so did not fear that I was about to die. I was more confused than anything else, and did not panic even when I heard the paramedic shout: 'Call an ambulance. Joe has had a stroke.' I was rushed to the Victoria Infirmary in Kirkcaldy, but I was still convinced that I had suffered some sort of minor turn and would be fine.

I did not realise how ill I was until I spoke to my children. Ross was abroad and called me by telephone shedding tears, and Laura and Joanna were also extremely upset when they visited the stricken patient. I did start to wonder if I might die, but the doctors reassured me, and I was fortunate that the stroke was considered minor. Lying in a hospital bed left time for much soul-searching though, and my evaluation of the important factors in life altered dramatically. I recalled how my children had been on at me constantly to slow down and not to undertake so many speaking engagements or personal appearances. They also urged me to take care of my diet and to drink less alcohol. At the age of 56 I was terrified that I might be paralysed down one side of my body for the rest of my life and become a burden to my family. I knew enough about strokes to be aware that they can recur; my life has revolved around Ross, Laura and Joanna, so I suppose it was a sad indictment of my thought processes that it took a stroke to make me realise that any time I have left with them is worth more than any goals I scored or glory I enjoyed as a professional footballer.

Since 2004 my priority has been to stay as fit as I can to ensure that I am around for a good few years yet, and I have cut back on dinner engagements: I want to *see* my children's lives progressing. Ross, who was 35 when I wrote this book, works as an estate agent in Glasgow and is a fine person. I reckon we are as close as a father and son can be, and I make a point of catching up with him and his partner Sarah as often as possible. Laura, 33, works with disadvantaged children in Glasgow and is pursuing a post-graduate course in teaching. She has always been a mother figure within the trio, and is one of the kindest individuals you could meet. She and her partner, Neil Thornton, are very happy together. Joanna, 31, works in the tourist industry, grading hotels for guides and magazines, and like her sister, is ever helpful. Chris is her long-term friend, and I, for one, would not complain if they became more than just pals. But that's none of my business. When contemplating my future I also considered my parents Eddie and Margaret, and I did not wish them to feel that their son had thrown his life away. My much-loved Aunt Sadie was also at the forefront of my thoughts. She speaks her mind, and so it came as no surprise that she did so with a vengeance after I suffered the stroke, but I appreciated the talking-to. My family rallied behind me when it was needed most, and the love and support they offered in my recovery proved invaluable.

I must say that I much appreciated the fact that my former wife Fiona was one of the first to visit me at hospital in Kirkcaldy. Our marriage not working out is one of the main regrets of my life, and I have always maintained that if I marry again it will be to the same woman. Fiona is a beautiful person and a fine mother to our children, and I reiterate that the fact they have grown to be such singular personalities is a testament to her. It pleases me that we have remained close friends, and Fiona can be assured that I will always be available if she needs help. I was also touched to receive visits in hospital from some of my old team-mates, including wee winger Bertie Miller. Former

Dons sprint coach Stuart Hogg popped by, and many pals, including best mate Ally Kennedy, trekked from Aberdeen. Co-author Charlie Allan and his wife Janice also travelled to Fife during the first few days of my recovery.

Charlie has a wicked sense of humour, and he cheered me by producing a copy of my 1980 testimonial brochure. 'Sign that,' he demanded. 'It could be the last thing you ever autograph – I could make a fortune on eBay!' I had been given a series of exercises to improve the coordination in my weakened right side, one involving laying six grapes in a line on a hospital bed tray then picking them up and eating them one by one. It seems a simple task, but in the weeks after I had suffered the stroke it was a painstaking process that took a lot out of me, and Charlie insisted that I give a demonstration during his visit. 'No point in wasting time,' he proclaimed, and chatted away while I took several minutes to lay the six grapes in a line. I was just about to start eating them when Charlie snatched them, and scoffed the lot! It made me laugh, which was something I had been missing. I also appreciated officials from Kennoway Bowling Club making the effort to visit me every day during my spell in hospital.

My partner Shiela is the person to whom I owe most in the aftermath of the stroke. She was my rock and drove from Aberdeen to Kirkcaldy every day. During one of her early hospital visits she discovered an envelope in an inside pocket of the jacket I had been wearing when I collapsed. It contained the fee that I had agreed with the Kennoway officials. When they visited I offered to return it, but they would have none of it, and we compromised with a deal that I would return to give a speech for no fee when I felt better. I was able to fulfil that promise a few months later, and on what proved to be a great night I began my address with: 'Now where was I . . .?' I followed that by dropping the microphone to the floor, and slight panic was apparent until the Fifers realised I was merely winding them up.

Sheila also took time off work to nurse me when I was finally allowed home. I could not have been cared for in a more loving manner, despite the fact that my concern over paralysis made me grumpy during the first few weeks of convalescence. The worry that I would be a long-term burden to Sheila was what terrified me most, though any prospect of feeling sorry for oneself was ruled out when I began to attend the stroke clinic at Aberdeen's Woodend Hospital. Many patients were far worse off than me, and I began to count my blessings and vowed to get as fit as possible. I marvelled at the hard work that Dr John Webster, assistant Katie and their staff put in to encourage so many stroke victims to take the road to recovery. I now do what I can to raise funds for their unit, for without their kind attention I doubt if my recovery would have been as rapid or as full.

I was delighted to be back to as near my best as I'm likely to get for my 60th birthday party in January 2008. My family gathered in Aberdeen with many former Dons team-mates, including Tommy McMillan, Drew Jarvie, Jim Whyte and John Hewitt, for a night to remember. And now that I have reached my seventh decade, I am still amazed at the warmth and affection shown to me by Aberdeen fans, even those born many years after I scored my last goal in 1979. Some make jokes about me having once slept with their mothers, or in some cases their grandmothers, but I love the jesting, which is why I never say no to requests for pictures or autographs. I have already stated that since suffering the stroke I have reduced my speaking diary. I still have a slight weakness down my right side and lots of aches and pains, and I take several pills to control blood pressure and treat other ailments, included regular bouts of gout. I tire easily and will normally be in bed by 9 p.m. unless I am due at a function, and I'm certainly not the whisky- and beer-drinking Joey the fans sang about all those years ago.

I was most touched to receive a load of letters of support from fans while I was recovering. Many said that they had been delighted by my contributions to Aberdeen Football Club, and I can assure them that I gained great pleasure from my service at Pittodrie. Whenever I venture in the Granite City, supporters still greet me as 'The King.' I bow at their feet in thanks for the significant part they played in making the footballing life of Joe Harper a very happy one.

21

WHAT THEY SAID ABOUT KING JOEY

'Pittodrie's Little and Large, all in one'

The following tributes were paid to me in 1980 when I was awarded a testimonial match by Aberdeen.

EDDIE TURNBULL (manager at Aberdeen and Hibernian)

'Joe was one of the best goal-snatchers to grace Scottish football.

He's King of the Beach End and thoroughly deserves it. I paid £40,000 to get him from Morton, and still reckon that was one of the best deals Aberdeen were ever involved in.'

ALEX FERGUSON (manager at Aberdeen)

'People don't realise the handicap Joe played under as a top player, his height. When you look at the strikers of the past, one thing stands out, they are all average to big in height and therefore scored a fair percentage of goals with their head. When you consider Joe scored 90 per cent or more with his foot only then you quickly realise why he has become a legend. But to class Joe as merely a striker is an injustice, because of all the players I have handled he has without doubt the sharpest brain. He sizes up situations before the balls land at his feet and knows exactly what he is going to do.'

ALLY MacLEOD (manager at Aberdeen and with Scotland)

'Bringing Joe back to Pittodrie was one of the best moves I made as a manager. He is not the physical image one normally associates with a footballer, but has an extraordinary talent that not many possess – the ability to score from the most unlikely of places. The scoring talent, allied to the Toby Jug look, forged an amazing relationship between Joe and the fans.'

BILLY McNEILL (opponent with Celtic and manager at Aberdeen)

'He is one of the best goal-scoring centre-forwards the Scottish game has produced. I had the greatest of respect for him as an opponent, who couldn't be given an inch of space or he was liable to find the net. During my spell as manager at Pittodrie I always found him a professional through and through and appreciated his abilities from a different relationship.'

JOE ROYLE (Everton team-mate)

'It's hard to recount any experiences with Joe that you can print.

I was injured when Joe first came to Everton, but I was immediately impressed by his goal sense. It was uncanny and, because I was out, he had little support, but still finished as Everton's top scorer. I was having my own problems, so didn't get to play alongside Joe as often as I would have liked.

Evertonians still ask me if the Harper-Royle partnership could have been a success. Given a better timing of affairs, the striking partnership of Big Joe and Little Joe could have been an unqualified success.'

ERIK SORENSEN (Morton team-mate)

'I remember Joe as a very young player who was eager to learn about the game and trained with Morton's Danish players every day. I also played with him in his very first game for Morton, against Partick Thistle, when he was only 16. Joe was up against George Niven and Donnie McKinnon, but marked his debut by scoring the only goal. Joe is a great wee player.'

HAL STEWART (manager at Morton)

'The first time I saw Joe I knew he was something special.

He was a natural and nothing ever curbed his enthusiasm to score goals.'

JIMMY BONTHRONE (manager at Aberdeen)

'You can place me at the top of the Joe Harper fan club. In my 30 years of involvement in the professional game few goal-scorers have impressed me as much as Joe. Joe played a leading role in Aberdeen's major successes and earned the right to be classed as one of the all-time greats.'

HARRY CATTERICK (manager at Everton)

'Joe is a born goal-scorer, which is why I purchased him for Everton.

He was unfortunate because he came when the team was breaking up after a successful run, so Joe never really had the chance to display his finishing ability. It was still a pleasure to work with such a remarkable goal-scorer.'

TOMMY DOCHERTY (manager with Scotland)

'I had no hesitation bringing Joe into my squad. He is a great little fellow, good fun and never let me down, on or off the pitch.

If I had remained Scotland manager I'm sure Joe would have become a regular in my team.'

JACK WEBSTER (author of the official Dons' history and journalist)

'Joe, as all the world knows, is King, the mighty monarch of Merkland Road, who rules over his empire with undisputed authority.'

EMLYN HUGHES (opponent with Liverpool)

'In my clashes with Joe I always found him a very difficult opponent to mark. He played football the way I liked it, with the intent to win.

When we faced each other we would often share a joke, depending on the score at the time. I must add it was usually in our favour!'

BOBBY CLARK (team-mate at Aberdeen)

'Nobody, and I mean nobody, beats Joe Harper easily. He hates to lose, be it at football, golf, table tennis, anything. That is why he was such a success, that tremendous determination to come out on top.'

PAT STANTON (opponent and team-mate with Hibs)

'Joe's goal-scoring feats speak for themselves. His talent for making the most of any opening puts him among a unique band of players.'

ALAN ROUGH (opponent with Partick Thistle, team-mate with Scotland)

'Joe was a goalkeeper's nightmare. You couldn't afford to make half-saves with him about. If you didn't take the ball cleanly he would dart in and pick up the scraps. He was also a ferocious competitor.'

DREW JARVIE (team-mate at Aberdeen)

'Pittodrie's Little and Large, all in one.'

STEVE ARCHIBALD (team-mate at Aberdeen)

'Wee Joe has the same attributes as Gerd Müller'

STUART KENNEDY (team-mate at Aberdeen)

'Wee Joe went to the same fitness farm as Liz Taylor!'

WILLIE MILLER (team-mate and captain at Aberdeen)

'Joe Harper means more to Aberdeen than North Sea oil.'

JOE HARPER

The Vital Statistics

CAREER COMPETITIVE RECORD

	Appearances	Goals
Morton (1963-67 and 1968-69):	85	65
Huddersfield Town (1967-68):	23	3
Everton (1972-74):	47	14
Hibernian (1974-75):	81	38
Aberdeen (1969-72 and 1975-80):	306	205
TOTALS	542	325

COMPLETE ABERDEEN RECORD

	Played	Goals
League:	207	126
League Cup:	51	51
Scottish Cup:	24	15
European Cup Winners' Cup:	6	3
UEFA Cup:	10	5
Anglo-Scottish Cup:	4	2
Drybrough Cup:	5	3
Friendly games:	57	37
TOTALS	364	242

INTERNATIONAL APPEARANCES
FULL CAPS

Appearances 4, goals 2.

October 18, 1973: Denmark (a) won 4-1 (Macari, Bone, Harper, Morgan)

Scotland: Clark, Brownlie, A Forsyth, Bremner, Colquhoun, Buchan, Lorimer, Macari (Dalglish), Bone (Harper), Graham, Morgan.

November 15, 1973: Denmark (h) won 2-0 (Dalglish, Lorimer).

Scotland: Harvey, Brownlie, Donachie, Bremner, Colquhoun, Buchan, Lorimer, Dalglish (Carr), Harper, Graham, Morgan.

September 3, 1975: Denmark (a) won 1-0 (Harper)

Scotland: Harvey, McGrain, A Forsyth, Bremner, McQueen, Buchan, Lorimer, Dalglish, Harper, Rioch, Hutchison (Duncan).

June 11, 1978: Iran (a) drew 1-1 (Eskandarian og).

Scotland: Rough, Buchan (T Forsyth), Jardine, Burns, Donachie, Macari Gemmill, Hartford, Jordan, Dalglish (Harper), Robertson.

UNDER-23 CAPS

Appearances 2.

January 14, 1970: Wales (h) 1-1 (O'Hare).

Scotland: Stewart, Clunie, Wilson, Blackley, Thomson, Campbell (Munro), Lorimer, Carr, O'Hare, Robb, Hartford (Harper).

January 13, 1971: Wales (a) 0-2.

Scotland: MacRae, Hay (Jardine), Hermiston (Oliver), Kelly, Munro, Buchan, Hartford, Carr, Harper, Connolly, Hutchison.

'UNOFFICIAL' WORLD TOUR APPEARANCES

Appearances 3, goals 8.

May 25, 1967: Hong Kong (a) 4-1 (Ferguson 2, Hood, Callaghan).

Scotland: Thomson, Callaghan, Colquhoun, Tinney (Townsend), Anderson, Fraser, Morgan, Hope (Harper), McCalliog, Ferguson, Hood.

June 5, 1967: New Zealand (a) 7-2 (Harper 3, McCalliog 2, McLean (pen), Lake og).

Scotland: Cruickshank, Callaghan (McCalliog), Tinney, Townsend, McGrory, Woodward, McLean, Penman, Harper, Hope, Hood.

June 13, 1967: Canada (a) 7-2 (Harper 5, Hope, Morgan).

Scotland: Cruickshank, Townsend, Tinney, Anderson, McGrory, Fraser (Penman), Morgan, Hope, Harper, Hood (McCalliog), McLean.

1964 EUROPEAN YOUTH CHAMPIONSHIPS FINALS

All matches in Holland – appearances 4, goals 3

Scotland 3 (Harper 2, McCalliog), Switzerland 1.

Scotland: Clark, Dickson, Smith, Watson, Fraser, Stevenson, Quinn, McCalliog, Harper, O'Rourke, Buckley.

Scotland 2 (Buckley, O'Rourke), Switzerland 0.

Scotland: Clark, Dickson, Smith, Watson, Fraser, Shepherd, Harper, O'Rourke, Lorimer, Stevenson, Buckley.

Scotland 2 (Stevenson, Buckley), Spain 3.

Scotland: Clark, Dickson, Smith, Watson, Fraser, Shepherd, O'Rourke, McCalliog, Harper, Stevenson, Buckley.

Scotland 2 (Harper, Buckley), Portugal 3.

Scotland: Clark, Dickson, Smith, Watson, Fraser, Shepherd, O'Rourke, McCalliog, Harper, Stevenson, Buckley.

SCOTTISH LEAGUE APPEARANCES – 2

TRANSFER TRAIL

May 1965 – Signed by Morton straight from school.

March 1967 – Sold to Huddersfield Town for £45,000.

September 1968 – Returns to Morton for £20,000.

October 1969 – Aberdeen sign him for a club record £40,000.

December 1972 – Sold to Everton for a record £180,000 fee.

February 1974 – Joins Hibs in a £120,000 deal.

April 1976 – Rejoins the Dons for £50,000.

TOTAL FEES: £455,000.

ABERDEEN'S LIST OF RECORD GOAL-SCORERS

	League	League Cup	Scottish Cup	Europe	Other	Total
1 Joe Harper:	125	51	15	8	6	205
2 Matt Armstrong:	134	0	19	0	5	158
3 George Hamilton:	101	33	18	0	4	156
4 Harry Yorston:	98	22	21	0	7	148
5 Drew Jarvie:	85	29	7	10	6	137
6 Benny Yorston:	102	0	24	0	0	126
7 Willie Mills:	102	0	13	0	3	118
8 Jackie Hather:	78	16	10	0	5	109
9 Davie Robb:	78	9	10	2	6	105
10 Mark McGhee:	60	18	6	14	3	101

INDEX

NB: initials JH in index indicate Joe Harper